THE COMPLETE GUIDE TO JACK RUSSELL TERRIERS

Kaylin Stinski

Publication Data

Kaylin Stinski
The Complete Guide to Jack Russell Terriers – First edition.
Summary: "Successfully raising a Jack Russell Terrier from puppy to old age"
– Provided by publisher.
ISBN: 978-1-954288-44-7
[1. Jack Russell Terriers – Non-Fiction] I. Title.

Design by Sorin Rădulescu
First paperback edition, 2022

TABLE OF CONTENTS

INTRODUCTION

My personal history with Jack Russell Terriers started while I was working in veterinary medicine. One of our clients had worked in Jack Russell rescue for years, and I often worked with her fosters, which gave me a well-rounded introduction to the breed. She then decided to transition into breeding. After my client's dog had its first litter, I knew that I wanted to add one to my home. Two years later, I reserved a pup.

Photo Courtesy of Kaylin Stinski

Being in the veterinary field, I was blessed with a full maternity experience. I got to see the pups in-utero on radiographs and ultra-sound. I got to see them a couple of days after they were born, again when they came in for their first exams, and when my puppy was weaned, he spent the night with me in the hospital as I was working on patients. He was born on October 30 and was given the name Goblin, which I promptly changed to Marty McFly, and he has been my constant companion since that night. Having a Jack Russell Terrier is no small feat; it can be very challenging at times, but I have never regretted opening my heart to one, and I look forward to sharing my experiences with you.

Photo Courtesy of Kaylin Stinski

CHAPTER ONE

The Origins of the Jack Russell Terrier Breed

History and origin

During the 19th century, Rev. John Russell created a strain of terriers from the Wire Fox Terrier and the Smooth Fox Terrier, and he perhaps even crossbred from Bull Terriers and Beagles, creating the Jack Russell Terrier Breed. The Rev. John Russell was an avid hunter who wanted a dog that could hunt foxes both above and below the ground.

In 1894, a breed standard was created by Arthur Blake Heinemann, but it wasn't until 1990 when the United Kingdom first recognized the breed as the Parson Jack Russell Terrier. In the United States, the breed was recognized as the Jack Russell Terrier in 1997. Eventually, the UK changed the name in 1999, and finally, by 2008, all international kennel clubs recognized the new name. To this day, there is still a strong divide between the American Kennel Club (AKC) and the Jack Russell Terrier Club of America (JRTCA) in their approach to the Jack Russell Terrier breed. These organizations have different breed standards and perspectives on what qualifies as a Jack Russell. The AKC has looser terms and standards when it comes to the breed and will register liters at birth. Sometimes these dogs are termed Parson Terriers, Russells, "shorties," or, potentially, a mix. The JRTCA, however, has very strict standards for their Jack Russell Terriers and is focused not only on the look of the dog but also how they work. Their goal is to protect, preserve, and work their terriers the way they were bred to be. Events promoted by the JRTCA are called trials, and they focus on the dog as a whole, focusing a lot on the drive and workability of the breed.

The JRTCA is a national breed club and registry in the United States that focuses on maintaining standards that aim to preserve the working-dog

*Photo Courtesy
of Nina Chang and Brooke Lloyd*

characteristics and the heritage of the Jack Russell Terrier breed. The organization was founded in 1976 and remains today as the largest Jack Russell Terrier registry and organization in the world. A large part of this organization focuses on the promotion, running, and sanctioning of national dog trials that are specific to the Jack Russell Terrier. Club affiliates will host Jack Russell Terrier trials and shows where the JRTCA will provide certified judges, and the winners of these shows and trials will move on to the annual national JRTCA competition. These events are attended by Jack Russell Terrier owners and breeders to compete in trial events and be judged to the breed standard.

The AKC did not recognize the Jack Russell Terrier until 1998. The American Kennel Club serves as an umbrella registry for a multitude of purebred dogs within the United States and is probably the most well-known registry in the country. For years, Jack Russell Terriers were not recognized by the AKC, and there was no Jack Russell Terrier breeder registry or available AKC-breed certification for owners to verify the authenticity of prospective dogs. A small group of JRTCA members asked the AKC to recognize the Jack Russell Terrier breed, which led to their recognition in 1998. However, the JRTCA thought that this recognition of the breed by the AKC was not in the best interest of the Jack Russell Terrier breed as a whole.

The JRTCA focuses on the working-dog characteristics and standards

Photo Courtesy of Julie Russon

of the breed and believes that recognition of the breed by the AKC would lead to a change in the breed towards show standards and lose the form and function of this working dog. The AKC certifies litters at birth by the pedigree of their parents, which does not consider the dogs' individual working instincts. On the other hand, the JRTCA requires the terrier to have reached one year of age, a traceable pedigree that is at least four generations deep, and a veterinarian's certification attesting to the dog's lack of inheritable defects. Only then can a dog be registered with the JRTCA.

The JRTCA is not strictly opposed to the AKC solely. In fact, the stance of the JRTCA is that all-breed registries, in general, are detrimental to the individual dog breeds but particularly detrimental to the Jack Russell Terrier. The JRTCA is a unique registry that has very strict restrictions on health requirements and inbreeding limitations. It also focuses on the breeder's code of ethics, which is designed to preserve the Jack Russell Terrier's unique working ability, intelligence, and sound physical structure in order to allow the safeguarding of Parson John Russell's working dog breed—the Jack Russell Terrier.

Marty McFly comes from a line of JRTCA recognized Jack Russell Terriers, and he has also participated in many JRTCA affiliated trials and shows. His story, my experience, and the writing of this book are aligned with the JRTCA's philosophy, ethics, and standards for the activities that surround the preservation of the Jack Russell Terrier breed.

Physical characteristics

The Jack Russell Terrier was bred to be about the size of a fox so it could "go to ground" and fit within the small burrows of foxes. This gives the dog a height between 10" and 15" at the shoulder. That's the perfect size for all sorts of travel and makes it easy for them to curl up on your lap while you're reading a book. Jack Russell Terriers can have a wide variety of coats—a rough, wiry coat, a soft, smooth coat, and a broken coat, which lies somewhere between rough and smooth.

The dogs have a double coat, which is weatherproof and can handle harsh conditions. However, having a double coat means that this breed does shed. My Jack Russell sheds a lot. We will get more into how that is managed in future chapters, but it is something to note if that may be of concern for you when selecting a dog. The primary color of a Jack Russell is usually white, accented by individual or mixed black and tan markings.

Though they are small in size, Jack Russells have relatively long legs compared to other terrier breeds, which allows them to pursue their prey on foot easily, or in my dog's case, to run through fields like a deer and look very cute while doing it. Their ears are really what tie their face together and give them their striking profile. The correct description of their ears would be "button," which means the ear folds forward.

Jack Russell tails are usually docked short a few days after their birth. Traditionally, the length of the tail should just be long enough to allow the handler or owner to pull the dog out of a fox's burrow. If you are considering competing with your Jack Russell, this is something to consider, as it is essentially for confirmation and is also an important tool in other sports. If you are not considering competing, docking is not necessary.

The coloration of the Jack Russell Terrier is a white base, and most Jack Russell Terriers are completely or predominately white with black, tan, or brown markings. Most kennel clubs will not penalize for having heavy body color, but the legs, chest, and belly must be white. Usually, the back and the sides are white and will have a few larger color markings, but if there is a significant amount of coloring, the dog may be ticked in order to see if white is the predominant color. Albinism is not accepted, as this is a recessive trait.

Behavioral characteristics

> **"**
>
> *Jack Russell Terriers do best in an environment where they have the opportunity to be active and engaged with their owners. Having a job or purpose along with plenty of human interaction and socialization is the ideal scenario. The worst possible environment for a JRT is one where the dog is isolated a great deal and doesn't have an outlet for its energy and intelligence. JRTs are always thinking, and when left without a way to use their mind, they will find their own way, and this usually results in trouble!*
>
> WENDY PALMER
> *Thistle Ridge Terriers*
>
> **"**

The Jack Russell Terrier is intensely loyal, affectionate, and a profound companion. When I say these dogs are like no other breed you've had before or any breed you will have again, I mean it. This breed wants to explore life with you and be your companion through everything. My Jack Russell is with me every moment he can be. Whether he is curled up on my lap, exploring hiking trails, or captaining my kayak, he is happy because he is with me. Now, they are a tenacious breed that can be sassy, but they also have courage, intelligence, a load of energy, and usually a strong hunting instinct.

One of the most important things to understand is that Jack Russell Terriers were bred to be hunting dogs. They are amazingly skilled at following scents, digging, barking and have been bred to show aggressive behavior if called for. A Jack Russell going after a fox in its den needs to be able to defend itself. These are important things to acknowledge even before adding a Jack to your home.

I was able to train a lot of this behavior out of my own Jack, but barking is one thing that I have never been able to get a full handle on. Their breeding also gives them a strong urge to follow a scent underground and bark at their quarry. This is part of what makes Jacks really good hunters, but if they do not have an outlet for this instinct, they can and will find alternate ways to entertain themselves.

Jack Russell Terriers are a fantastic example of the Napoleon complex; they are big dogs in tiny bodies. Part of this directly involves their need for exercise. They tend to need the amount of exercise you would expect from a large dog.

FUN FACT

Jack Russell Terrier Club of America (JRTCA)

The Jack Russell Terrier Club of America (JRTCA) is the National Breed Club for Jack Russells in America. It was founded in 1976 and is affiliated with the Jack Russell Terrier United World Federation (JRTUWF). The JRTCA is not affiliated with the American Kennel Club (AKC) and includes members from the United States, Canada, England, Scotland, Australia, and more. It is the largest Jack Russell Terrier club and registry in the world. For more information about the club, visit www.therealjackrussell.com/jrtca.

They are also often fearless and have been known to challenge multiple dogs at a time. This is a breed that truly believes it has the same might and power as a 150-pound dog. Sometimes this mindset can lead to aggressive behavior, which is something all individuals should consider before investing in this breed.

My Marty Mcfly is the gentlest dog. He has not ever bitten a person or a dog in his life. But if I am sitting on the couch watching TV with him lying next to me, and another dog comes up to get love, Marty McFly will growl at them to leave. This is still aggressive behavior and is something to consider, especially if you have other dogs in your home.

Along the same lines of this strong personality is the fact that many Jack Russell dogs become possessive of their owner or the individual they connect with the most. This can escalate to aggressive behavior and should be corrected early on. When my boyfriend moved in, Marty McFly would jump up on the couch, cross my boyfriend's lap, and lie in between us, looking at him as if to say, "I have been here way longer than you, so know your place." Though cute, this is a possessive behavior that I had to correct in order to make sure it did not escalate into something worse.

Is a Jack Russell a good fit for your home?

> "
>
> *The best owner profile would be someone who is intelligent, understands and enjoys structure and rules, and enjoys energy and activity. Jack Russells can be great with a single adult...they love your company and time. They do well in homes with children IF the children are well trained and respectful...If you can raise a pleasant child, you will love a Terrier. Retirees can also be good for JRTs because they have the time and desire to train and challenge a young puppy into adulthood. Perhaps the best answer would be the kind of home or lifestyle that is not suited for a Jack...I rarely place puppies in homes that have a collection of dogs and/or companion animals or who believe they are a good match just because they live on acres of land 'to run.*
>
> SUE ANNE WILSON
> *West Elk Terriers*
>
> "

The Jack Russell Terrier has a demanding personality, and this is not a breed that can be a backyard dog or a mellow couch potato. There are a lot of individuals, with or without previous dog ownership experience, that become overwhelmed by this breed. This often leads to dogs becoming abandoned, often before they reach full maturity. I also experienced very frustrating periods of time the first few years with Marty McFly that left me wondering whether I made the right choice.

When considering getting a Jack Russell, you should note the following:

- **They are bred to hunt** – As discussed in the behavior section, Jack Russells have been bred to hunt, dig, bark, and, in general, get themselves into trouble. This means that when considering a Jack Russell, it is also important to consider what you want to do with your dog. Is he going to become your running buddy, or are you both going to explore a new dog sport? Whatever you decide, your dog will need a job to do!

- **They are bred to hold their own, above and below ground** – When these tiny dogs go down a hole in pursuit of quarry, they need to be able to hold their own, and they absolutely do. This also relates to domestic, non-hunting life. Often when I brought my Jack Russell to the dog park, one big 80-pound goofy dog wouldn't understand his size and would start picking on him. The dog would paw at him, push him around, and poke him with his nose. My Jack would try to be patient and warn the dog, but after a few minutes of this, he would let the dog know that he was annoyed by snapping and holding his own against something eight times his size.

Photo Courtesy of Jacqueline Robson

- **Talk about a Napoleon complex** – Though Jacks may be little, they are strong! Often they forget they are small dogs, and they are fearless in all things. This personality trait often gets them in trouble if unchecked.

- **They have a possessive personality** – A Jack Russell's possessiveness can cause conflict within the home and outside of it. Usually, a Jack Russell will connect with an individual and become very possessive of that person. This possession can lead to aggression toward other dogs, cats, and even other people. My little Marty McFly is particularly obsessed with me, and this is a behavior I have to consistently discourage to prevent it from escalating into something worse.

- **They have the potential for aggression toward other dogs** – A lot of Jack Russell-specific websites will mention that this breed is aggressive to dogs of the same sex and that Jacks show aggression to other dog breeds. Though this has a significant amount of truth to it, I have not had this experience. Marty McFly grew up with two Border Collies who were also male, just like him. They were his closest friends. Even after they passed, whenever Marty McFly met another Border Collie, he became all excited and happy because that breed is what he associated his family with.

- **They can harass smaller animals** – The Jack Russell Terrier was bred to go after small game, and that is still ingrained in their brains. This often leads to harassment of other small pets like cats, birds, or rodents. Again, this can depend on the individual dog. I have seen my dog have a cat for a best friend and literally run away from street cats in terror, but at the same time, lunge after birds during walks like they are his mortal enemies.

■ **They need strong and consistent training throughout their life** – Jacks are very intelligent dogs that will always test their limits to see what they can get away with. Before their owners realize it, Jack Russell Terriers will train them, and because the breed can be so assertive, it is important to maintain expectations and standards for your Jack Russell's behavior.

■ **They require training** – All dogs require training, but the Jack Russell has such a strong hunting instinct that basic training is needed and may even save your dog's life. The breed is known to follow their nose, and if you do not have a good recall or "leave-it" command, your Jack may disappear into the woods or down a hole, and you may not see your dog again.

■ **Their coats will shed, so be prepared** – This breed sheds, and you will find the hair everywhere, no matter what type of coat they have. This is just the way life goes with a Jack Russell. If shedding is something you don't want to deal with, you may want to consider a different breed.

■ **They will get bored and can become destructive** – Exercise, activity, and companionship are vital things to maintain a good relationship with your dog. When one or more of these factors are not being addressed, the stubborn side of Jacks will come out, and it tends to be destructive.

■ **They are not tolerant most of the time** – Again, this is a dog that is very assertive and demanding. Jacks tend not to have a lot of patience, and this can be an issue in many families. If you have children or are thinking of having children in the future, be aware that a lot of training and consistent standards of behavior must be maintained in order to prevent issues.

■ **They are not what the media portrays them as** – I grew up watching Wishbone, and as an adult, I realized very quickly that Wishbone must have had a ton of training. The movies and shows portray Jack Russells solely on their best behavior.

■ **They are country dogs at heart** – This simply means that Jack Russells have energy to burn, and staying cooped up in an apartment all day will not end well for anybody. A large home or an active companion is necessary to keep a Jack Russell happy and non-destructive.

■ **They require a lifetime commitment** – Many Jack Russell Terriers live for 15 years or more and will need to have activity, entertainment, and companionship for the extent of their life. While it's definitely work caring for a Jack, the relationship and connection between the two of you will be beyond measure.

Photo Courtesy of Rebecca Allan

I know this sounds like a lot of negatives, but I want to make sure you have the full picture before you commit to a Jack Russell. During my first two years with Marty McFly, I had a lot of hard times trying to address his behaviors. Years later, we have created a relationship so deep that words cannot even begin to describe it, but it took time. He is my best friend and my forever adventure buddy. We hike, backpack, kayak, and spend every moment possible together. Nothing is more rewarding than coming home to your best friend every day.

CHAPTER TWO
Finding Your Jack Russell

> "
>
> *Don't fall for the allure of the JRT's markings or coat type! If the breeder or rescue agent really knows their dogs, they will give you recommendations on which dog or puppy is best suited for your lifestyle. Listen to them. I match the puppy to the job or household. It's important to work with someone who has the main goal of putting each dog or puppy in the most successful environment and not just moving them on as fast as possible. Markings are only cute for so long. It is the right temperament and level of drive for your lifestyle that will make a happy dog and family for the next 15+ years.*
>
> WENDY PALMER
> *Thistle Ridge Terriers*
>
> "

Adoption vs. buying from a breeder

Deciding whether to adopt or buy a Jack Russell Terrier from a breeder is a big decision and one I personally debated when I was first considering the breed. The Jack Russell is a breed that is going to be challenging no matter where you get your puppy or adult dog from. This is a highly personal choice, and there are strong advocates on both sides of the spectrum.

I decided to go with a breeder because I wanted to start from scratch. I knew I wanted a puppy; I knew I was going to try and compete with my dog. This was my first time with a Jack Russell, so I didn't feel experienced enough to handle adopting a dog that might have behavioral issues beyond my skill

Photo Courtesy of Rebecca Allan

set. Part of this worked out, but part of this did not, and I feel it was a very narrow mindset, looking back.

First of all, consider what age you want your dog to be. Do you want a puppy, or would you like a dog that is a little more mature? If you feel you want to take on the "start from scratch" mindset, you are not limited to just a breeder. There are many puppies that come into rescues that will give you that new slate you are looking for. However, if you are looking to compete with your Jack Russell under organizations that require a breed certificate, such as American Kennel Club conformation events—think Westminster— then you will need to get your puppy from a breeder.

If a puppy is something you are not interested in, consider an older Jack Russell Terrier. Many people who get a Jack Russell without doing the proper background research find themselves overwhelmed by the breed and either return the dog to the breeder or send it to a rescue organization or humane facility. This can be a blessing in disguise for you because an older dog may already be housebroken and/or spayed or neutered and will most likely already have its puppy vaccines. Getting an adult Jack Russell from a breeder or a rescue organization is a good path to consider because the dog is being raised by someone who knows the breed, loves it, and can work with its unique behaviors.

Cost of adoption vs. buying from a breeder

The cost of adopting vs. buying from a breeder can be vastly different, and though some people say cost shouldn't matter, I find sometimes it does. Adoption is always going to be the most cost-effective route unless you are personal friends with a breeder and can get a discount. Full disclosure, I got a friend discount because I worked in veterinary medicine and had been seeing my breeder's dogs for years.

Below is a breakdown of the average costs of adopting versus buying a puppy. These are averages, and the actual costs may be different in your location.

■ **Adoption costs:**

- Adoption fees usually range from $75 - $250, depending on the organization and the location.
  - Most often, this fee includes:
    ‣ Initial puppy vaccination series
    ‣ The cost of spaying or neutering
    ‣ Dog license (depending on the organization)
    ‣ Microchipping
    ‣ Basic prevention such as flea and tick and heartworm prevention
    ‣ Sometimes this also includes other medical care done prior to adoption, if there is a previous injury that needed to be fixed or a medical condition that needed to be treated. These are often addressed by the organization and will need to be considered if further or long-term care is needed, such as with a diabetic dog.

■ **Cost to buy from a breeder:**

- ■ $400 - $2,500, depending on the breeder and heritage of the dog's parents.
  - • Initial vaccines – worth $20-$40
  - • Any tail docking – worth $10 - $20
  - • Health screens may or may not be paid for by breeder – worth $100 - $500
- ■ $50 - $300 for spaying or neutering
- ■ $75 - $125 to complete vaccine series
- ■ $50 for a microchip

Whether you choose to adopt or to buy from a breeder, there will also be long-term costs for your dog. Healthy dogs need to have annual examinations with vaccines and sometimes blood work; there are monthly preventative medications that need to be given and the cost of food, treats, toys, and training. In addition to these costs are the costs that come with aging dogs and the costs of unexpected events that lead to unscheduled veterinary visits.

Finding a reputable rescue organization

There are a variety of different places where you can find a Jack Russell Terrier to adopt. There are Jack Russell Terrier-specific rescue organizations, Terrier rescues, general rescue organizations, and humane societies. In all of these locations, you may find the Jack Russell of your dreams, but we will guide you through the pros and cons of these different types of organizations and how to discern which organization is reputable.

- **Jack Russell Terrier Rescues (Breed-Specific Rescues)**

Jack Russell Terrier Rescues are breed-specific rescues that will only rescue dogs that look like Jack Russell Terriers or look like they may be a Jack Russell Terrier Mix. These rescues are great because they focus on the breed itself and are usually run by people who are very passionate about the breed and have a deep understanding of what their rescues need in order to succeed in a home. This is a great place to start when looking to adopt a Jack Russell.

- **Terrier Rescues (Class-specific)**

There are some terrier rescues that don't focus on one specific breed but on the whole terrier group itself. This means there is more diversity in the dogs that they have available, but they all come from the same type of background and are similar in behavior to Jack Russells.

- **General Rescues (Non-specific rescues)**

General rescues don't have any restrictions on the breed of dog, but that doesn't mean they are any less reputable. There are a lot of rescues that are based on location, and they take in relinquished dogs and rescue them from local shelters or from areas that are overpopulated with dogs. They are usually run by people who are very passionate about rescue and may have a deep understanding of dog behavior, though they may have less breed-specific knowledge.

- **Humane Societies/Shelters (Non-rescue)**

Humane societies and shelters are usually where stray dogs go and are kept until their owner comes to pick them up or they get adopted. These locations are prone to euthanizing their animals at higher rates, depending on the organization. There tends to be less knowledge of the individual dogs themselves, and you may not have any background on the dog at all.

When looking into organizations to adopt from, there are some things that I recommend researching in order for you to have the best adoption experience and support after you bring your new family member home.

> ### ➢ Are they a registered non-profit 501(c)3 organization?

Registered 501(c)3 organizations are not-for-profit organizations, which means that the majority of the organization's financials, adoption fees, and donations should go directly toward the care of the rescue dogs themselves. If an organization claims to be a non-profit rescue but does not have a 501(c)3 status, inquire why not. They may just be waiting for the paperwork to be approved, but if they can't provide a statement of pending status, the organization may be one to avoid.

> ### ➢ Do they have transparent financials or end-of-year reports?

End-of-year reports usually detail the work an organization has accomplished throughout the last fiscal year and often discuss the total number of adoptions, donations, and where that money went to. Not all organizations do end-of-year reports, but there should be some financial transparency on their website, or it should be presented to you upon request. If they are unable to disclose this information, you may want to find another organization.

> ### ➢ What are their adoption policies?

This is one of the most important aspects to consider when looking into an organization. Most adoption policies are a binding contract between you and the organization for the benefit of the dog. It should state that the organization is providing the healthiest dog to its knowledge and has disclosed any previous medical history or health/behavioral issues. The contract will state something along the lines that you are committing to providing a home within a standard environment (fenced yard, etc.). See contracts and agreements for more information.

> ### ➢ Do they have a trial period?

This is something to consider when looking at organizations because it gives you some time with the dog in your home environment to see how he settles in and works with your family dynamic. Usually, once people find a dog that they love, they go through the whole adoption process, but the adoption fee is held for a certain amount of time in case something doesn't work out.

> ➤ **Are they available post-adoption for support?**

Having support from the organization after adoption is beneficial because it allows for continued care training of the rescue. Being able to reach out to the foster parent to discuss a behavior you are seeing and how they would recommend addressing it allows for a long-term relationship with your dog and doesn't leave you feeling lost or alone in training.

Finding a reputable breeder

When it came to my breeder, I was very lucky because I had already built a relationship with her before I decided to purchase my Jack Russell. She was a vital tool in my toolbox after I had brought him home and for many years after. To this day, when I post something on social media about him, good or bad, she is there. When my dog got diagnosed with a rare disease, the breeder reached out to me to discuss everything in order to see if this was something in her genetic line or a one-off event. She cared about maintaining the breed for its original purpose and was passionate about her dogs going to the best homes.

Some of Marty McFly's siblings didn't do well in placements, and the breeder took them back after a lot of counseling and training of the owners. She rehomed the dogs and followed their progress throughout their life. That is what, in my personal opinion, makes a good breeder. However, there are also other, more specific criteria that are good indicators of a reputable breeder.

- **Are they members of the Jack Russell Terrier Club of America (JRTCA)?**

The Jack Russell Terrier Club of America (JRTCA) is an organization that is deeply focused on preserving the working heritage and the unique characteristics that make up the Jack Russell Terrier. They were founded in 1976 and have continued to strive toward the protection of this breed, focused not on whole litters but on individual puppies, judging each dog from each litter and generation by its individual merits. A breeder who is a member of this organization is more inclined to share these same values.

- **Have they signed the JRTCA Breeders code of ethics?**

A breeder who has signed the JRTCA Breeders Code of Ethics has committed to the breed, its offspring, and the greater Jack Russell community.

This code of ethics is also a commitment to you as the potential new owner. It is important to read over the code of ethics to gain a deeper understanding of the breeder's role and what they should be providing you as the buyer.

● Can you meet the breeder?

Absolutely a must. Meeting the breeder, meeting the litter, and taking a puppy home does not all happen in one day, and that is a good thing. These commitments take time, and a relationship is being built between you and the breeder. The meeting doesn't have to be face to face; a phone call or other method is fine. Personally, I like to meet the breeder, see their facility or home, and get a full understanding of the environment my potential new dog is coming from. This is not feasible in all cases, but good judgment and gut feelings are good indicators as well.

● Can you meet the parents of the litter?

More often than not, you will only be able to meet one of the parents, usually the mother, but not both of them. This is because some breeders do not own both the father and the mother of the litter. However, do ask about meeting the parents, and make sure to clarify the background of each parent.

● Do they provide a full medical history of the litter and parents?

The litter itself may not have an extensive medical history, if any at all, but some things may be included, such as testing and health certificates, vaccines, whether any of the puppies in the litter died, etc. The medical history of the parents will give you more insight into the long-term health of your potential new puppy.

Photo Courtesy of Nina Chang and Brooke Lloyd

● Do they provide documentation of pedigree?

This should be presented before you purchase a puppy. This is like a family tree for your puppy and allows you to see his lineage and what titles were won if your puppy comes from a line of competitors.

- **Do they require a contract?**

Not only should breeders require a contract, but there should be certain details within the contract that talk about their commitment to you and your future puppy, as well as the expected commitment from you to the breeder and the puppy. This also goes back to the JRTCA Code of Ethics and is a good resource to look for contract expectations. Many people who breed for money, also known as "backyard breeders," do not have such a contract.

Health tests and certifications

Most of the health tests listed below are in reference to the breeding parents of the puppy you are considering. Both parents should be tested and certified prior to breeding, and there are specific timelines that must be upheld. These can be found in the JRTCA Code of Ethics. These tests are also something to consider when adopting a Jack Russell to give you a better understanding of the health of your pet throughout his lifetime. If you do end up adopting a Jack Russell Terrier, discuss these tests with your veterinarian to see which ones would be most beneficial for your dog.

Brainstem auditory evoked response (BAER) test:

This test is done in order to assess and evaluate the hearing of dogs. It takes a full look at the components used to hear, from the external ear canal to the middle/inner ear cavities, and even looks into the cranial nerve and some areas of the brainstem.

Companion animal eye registry (CAER) examination:

This examination provides breeders with information regarding any canine eye diseases that may or may not be present in order to give the breeder the ability to make informed decisions about breeding to produce healthier puppies. This examination was once referred to as a CERF examination, but the term has since been updated.

Primary lens luxation (PLL) vision testing:

This is a DNA test that assesses the likelihood of lens luxation, which can lead to uveitis or the development of glaucoma. Usually, these result in painful, teary red eyes that may look hazy or cloudy.

Spinocerebellar ataxia (SCA) testing:

This is a DNA test to assess a dog's potential for developing spinocerebellar ataxia, which is commonly found in Jack Russell Terriers. This affects a dog's ability to run, and it develops a goose-stepping gait, which makes the dog's legs appear as if they are going every which way.

Canine degenerative myelopathy (DM) tests:

This test evaluates whether the individual dog is normal, a carrier, or at risk for the disease. If a dog develops DM, it will develop weakness that gets progressively worse, starting as a wobble while walking, then knuckling or dragging of the feet, and eventually, the dog will become weak to the point that it can no longer walk.

Contracts and guarantees

Contracts and guarantees can be vastly different between a breeder and an adoption organization. Both usually discuss the responsibility that new owners are going to take on by adding a new dog to their home. They will discuss the condition of the dog itself, discuss the sale or adoption fee and what is included in that, and what should occur if the dog can no longer stay in the new owner's home (usually resulting in a return to the breeder or the rescue organization.)

■ **Breeding contracts should:**

- Disclose any information about genetic conditions in the parents or the ancestry.

- Accurately represent the qualities of their terriers without misleading prospective buyers.

- Include a policy regarding unregistrable terriers (if registering with the JRTCA).

- Include a clause that if, at any time, the Jack Russell owner cannot keep the dog, the dog must be returned to the breeder, or another arrangement must be made with the breeder's consent.

- Note in the contract any requirement for spaying/neutering, usually due to genetics.

- Be clear and concise contracts that are signed and dated by both parties.

■ **Adoption contracts:**

- Usually include a description of the adoption fee, most often referred to as an adoption donation. This description should also disclose what is covered under the adoption fee, spay/neuter, vaccines current for the estimated age of the dog, and a microchip.

- Sometimes a puppy is too small to be spayed or neutered before adoption, so this may be included in the contract to ensure that the dog comes back or gets spayed/neutered within a specific time period.

- A commitment to long-term veterinary care of the adopted dog should be included in any adoption contract. This just puts on paper that you will continue to care for the dog, and it also discloses any prior treatment. In addition, there is usually a line that states that the organization is adopting out a dog that is healthy to the best of their knowledge unless otherwise noted. Usually, this is referring to a dog that has a chronic illness like arthritis or diabetes, which will require continued veterinary care.

- Training is sometimes part of a contract, and this is usually just another way for new owners to show their commitment to the dog.

- Return policies are usually placed in the contract for general returns or returns based on behavioral issues.

- Oftentimes there are other agreements, such as always having identification on your dog, when euthanasia is appropriate, and a release of liability.

- The contract/agreement should be signed by the adopter and a member of the organization.

Photo Courtesy of Shelby Queen

Choosing your pup

> "
>
> *You need to expect a Jack Russell to live well into its late teens, so you need to find a dog who is healthy, with an outgoing personality. Genetics do play a role in personality and temperament. You can train a lot of behavior, but some issues are inherited. If purchasing from a breeder, try to share as much as possible about YOUR lifestyle, so the breeder, who knows the dogs or puppies the best, can help choose the dog that will best fit you. If you go to a rescue, find out as much as you can about the dog's history... does it flee/run, bite, submissive pee, bark, lack social skills with other animals, or show aggression in any situations? Is it used to a family, or was it a companion to a senior who had to give the dog up? Expect a bit longer of a honeymoon or adjustment period when taking a Jack Russell from a shelter...they appreciate human attention but need structure to be able to understand rules and expectations.*
>
> SUE ANNE WILSON
> *West Elk Terriers*
>
> "

If you have made it this far, it is safe to assume you are truly committed to adding a Jack Russell to your home. Congratulations! All the background work has been done. You have decided on the age, the gender, whether you are going to adopt or go through a breeder, and now you are ready to start your search. Here comes the really fun part—meeting all the puppies and dogs to see which one will become your newest addition.

When you start doing meet and greets, there are a few ways to go about this, but here are some key things to look for while meeting the puppies and dogs.

• Go alone

If you are the one who is looking to get the dog, I recommend visiting by yourself. If you don't have a good feeling or there is a disconnect, then there is no reason to drag the rest of the family to the breeder or rescue. For puppies, I like to meet the whole litter at once without my partner, friends, or family there because I like to make my own assessment first, then ask for other opinions.

FUN FACT
Recent Addition

Jack Russell Terriers were only recently recognized by the American Kennel Club (AKC) as a breed in 2012. The Kennel Club gave this breed full recognition in Britain in 2016. As of 2021, the Jack Russell is the 82nd most popular breed out of 200 to be registered with the AKC. Jack Russell Terriers were the 175th breed to be registered with the AKC.

- **Observation**

Observing how the dog acts alone and with other dogs is important because it gives you insight into the dog's personality. Does he love to play with toys by himself? Does he like to chase other dogs? Is he outgoing and playful? Simply by stepping back and observing, you can learn a lot about a dog and a puppy.

With Marty McFly, I sat on the floor with the breeder and the veterinarian for a solid hour when they came in for their initial veterinary examination and testing. We all sat in a circle, allowing the puppies to crawl all around and all over us. I knew I wanted a boy. As we sat, I watched Marty McFly, Goblin then, nestle into our laps and pay attention to the conversation. Whoever was talking, he would look at and continue to follow the conversation. This is what drew me to him, his connection and focus with humans. I looked for this because I wanted to compete in agility with him, and there is a need for that connection.

- **Get hands-on**

When meeting a dog or a puppy, I always make sure to place my hands all over the dog. I like to touch the ears, put my fingers inside the mouth, rub the gum lines, touch the paws, grab the tails gently, and see how each dog responds. Most puppies will just try to pull away or get your finger out of their mouth. But if they try to bite or nip, I know this needs to be addressed and that the dog's patience threshold is very low. In older dogs, it is the same concept, but they may have a stronger reaction. If you are not comfortable with doing this, ask the breeder, veterinarian, or kennel staff to demonstrate for you.

- **Meet the rest of the human family**

This allows everyone else to get a feel for the potential new addition. This is especially important for rescues because they have an unknown background and may have idiosyncrasies that are unknown until a dog has to face them. For example, the dog may love people but could start barking at someone with a beard. It's good to see if your potential new dog is not only good for you but your family as a whole.

- **Meet the rest of the animal family**

If possible, introduce any pets you already have to the new addition to see how they react. The best way to do this is in a neutral area that neither of the dogs is familiar with. Some rescues have separate areas that are only used for meet and greets. It is good to make sure this is done in an enclosed space and on leash or in separate fenced-in areas so that both dogs can be contained and separated but still introduce themselves. If this goes well, they can be introduced in the same space. Make sure to follow the rescue or organization's guidelines when doing such introductions.

This is usually for two adult dogs meeting, but I like to do this for older puppies as well.

- **Trial run**

Some organizations and rescues will allow you to take the dog into your home for a trial run that can be just an overnight excursion or, in some cases, up to two weeks. This is to see how the potential new addition does inside your home and in your natural environment. It is really hard to see a rescue dog's personality in a kennel or a run, and they tend to blossom more when they are in a home environment.

A trial run is usually never done with puppies from breeders because of the liability.

- **Do you have that feeling?**

In the end, if all the boxes are checked and a dog seems like it fulfills your wants, but you don't have that gut feeling, then don't go for it. That feeling is that connection, that understanding in your marrow that this is your dog. It bubbles up in you and makes you confident in yourself and the choice you are about to make. Again, this is from personal experience, and "that feeling" may be different for everyone, but as they say, if you know, you know!

CHAPTER THREE

Preparing Your Home for Your Jack Russell Terrier

> **"**
>
> *Jack Russells are a very special breed. They require someone who understands they were originally bred primarily as hunting dogs. They were required to think independently when introduced to quarry underground. With this in mind, a family that respects the JRT's disposition to think things through is desirable. An active or semi-active family with a fenced backyard is also desirable. Apartment life is not recommended unless the owner can provide ample daily exercise. Jack Russells do best when included in your daily activities as well.*
>
> ELLIE THOMPSON
> *Shavano Creek JRT*
>
> **"**

Family dynamics; where does your Jack Russell fit in?

Though Jack Russell Terriers are a headstrong breed, they can make terrific family pets. Jack Russell Terriers have a gentle and kind side that makes them wonderful companions that can get along with children and other pets. Many are friendly with small children, as long as the child has been educated on how to properly handle a terrier. This is an important distinction because though Jack Russell Terriers can be patient and kind, there is a limit, and they will not put up with harassment. This should be carefully considered

if you have a home with very small children.

Jack Russell Terriers love to have human attention and will seek it in all shapes and forms. Due to their assertive nature, you may find that your dog may start training you in order to get the attention he wants. I found with my Jack Russell that he wanted to be a princess, and a few months, later I realized that I had a bed for him in every room, and wherever I went, there he was with a princess palace waiting for him. Though I didn't mind beds everywhere, my whole house was changed to accommodate Marty McFly. This is an important lesson to take. Boundaries need to be set and maintained in order to create a happy home environment.

While the breed is very adaptable to multiple environments, Jack Russells are born and bred to hunt, so they have high energy and intelligence that both need to be exercised. This can be very challenging in an apartment environment or within a city unless you take serious strides to satiate the dog's needs. That being said, it is possible to have a Jack Russell in an apartment, but it takes work. I live in New York City, and my Jack Russell has been plenty happy there, but this does not come easily. He and I take at least three walks a day, one encompassing multiple miles on the beach playing fetch and digging for crabs. We also have a small, shared backyard to play in and spend many days kayaking out on Jamaica Bay together, where he goes swimming in the water. He gets plenty of attention while walking on the boardwalk, and I work from home, so whatever he needs, I am there to play, cuddle, and entertain.

Within your family unit, your Jack Russell will more than likely pick favorites, and everyone else will fall in descending order after. This does not mean the dog will not interact or play with anyone else, but he will choose who he prefers to interact with, and if that individual is not available, the dog will go down the line to the next on the list, and so on and so forth. When the dog's favorite person returns home, he will head straight for that individual. Unlike parents, Jack Russell Terriers choose favorites, and you will know it.

Puppy-proofing (or new dog-proofing) your home

> *If a Jack Russell does anything wrong the first year...it is the people's fault. Don't leave your favorite shoes where the dog can find them. Provide a place or way for the dog to go to the bathroom and remove clutter from the floor as much as possible. Have a 'safe' location set up for the puppy or adult dog. It should be a wire crate, playpen, or restricted area where he can be safely located when he is not being supervised, needs to rest, or needs a timeout. This area should not be used as a punishment but rather as a space that is the canine's, where it can chew a bone, play with a toy, or rest. Outside areas need to be checked so that fences are secure both in height and at the ground. Once a Terrier finds a way out, it will remember and use it again. Do frequent checks of any confinement. Terriers get bored easily, and digging is their claim to fame...give them one area where that is allowed, so they do not destroy the whole yard. Installing a chain-link-type kennel run with a doghouse is a good way to give a Jack Russell safe time outside without being controlled by his human the whole time. When the owner is present, that is when the Terrier is allowed into the common space and should be encouraged to play and be with his people.*
>
> SUE ANNE WILSON
> *West Elk Terriers*

If you have never had a dog before, the following is a great guide to make sure you have done your best to prepare your home for the new arrival. If this is not your first rodeo, this section may be good just to review to make sure you haven't forgotten anything. The goal of puppy-proofing your home is to make sure that you provide a safe environment and prevent access to anything that might be dangerous. This protects both your puppy and your home.

Photo Courtesy
of David Rainbow

Indoor environmental considerations

> *Preparing for a Jack Russell is initially much the same as preparing your home for a human toddler—especially a puppy. Make sure small objects that might be swallowed are put away, plugs and cords are tucked in, and favorite shoes and handbags are completely out of reach. A Jack Russell puppy is a force to be reckoned with and will challenge you in many different ways. Be patient, as this phase lasts only a few months, and the rewards are a well-rounded and loyal Terrier.*
>
> ELLIE THOMPSON
> *Shavano Creek JRT*

Electrical cords

▸ Electrical cords pose a risk to your puppy. They can cause electrical burns or may even provide an electrical shock. It is important to disconnect and put away electrical cords that are not being used and place cord protectors over cords that are accessible to your pup.

Cleaning supplies/potentially toxic substances

▸ Cleaning supplies should be put away in a cabinet that your puppy or dog cannot get into. Any spilled chemicals should be cleaned up immediately. It is also advisable to look at the labels of your cleaning supplies to see if they are pet safe. Dogs can absorb chemicals through their paws and also tend to lick floors, which can cause them to ingest something that may be toxic to them.

Medications

▸ Keeping medications out of reach of dogs is very important because many human medications can cause severe organ damage, failure, or death in dogs. Keeping medications on a countertop is not safe because dogs can still reach them if they decide to "counter surf." The best place to keep meds is in a cabinet with a door.

Photo Courtesy
of Brenda Foraie

Toilet lids

> ▸ Many toilet bowl cleaners are toxic to dogs and may cause chemical burns in a dog's mouth or on its tongue. Closing toilet lids will protect your dog and will also prevent him from drinking from the toilet bowl.

Window blinds and curtains

> ▸ Blinds and curtains may be interesting toys for curious pups and dogs who don't know that they shouldn't chew or play with such things. When settling a dog into its new home, it is advisable to tuck these out of reach until the dog is better trained.

Remove non-dog-friendly objects

> ▸ The category of non-dog-friendly objects covers a lot of things, but it includes things that puppies and dogs are still learning they can or cannot play with. Some of the most important objects to teach your dog to distinguish between are clothing garments, especially socks and underwear, and other fabric materials because they can be very similar to fabric-based toys. Especially for the first couple of weeks or months, puppies and dogs need to be closely supervised inside because they may ingest something that will not pass through their gastrointestinal system, and this can lead to emergency surgery.

Secure trash cans

> ▸ For the same reason described above, trash cans can hold tons of potentially toxic things and things that can get stuck in a puppy's or dog's intestines and can lead to emergency veterinary care. Most importantly, take the trash out when there are appetizing objects in there, such as a chicken carcass or any bones.

Houseplants

> ▸ Almost all houseplants can cause gastrointestinal upset in dogs, lots of salivating, vomiting, or diarrhea if ingested, especially in large quantities. Some houseplants can also cause neurological issues such as seizures. It is important to keep houseplants out of reach and also look into what effects the plant may have if ingested. The Pet Poison Hotline is a great resource that can be reached by phone at (855) 764-7661 or online at https://www.pet-poisonhelpline.com/poisons/.

Outdoor environmental considerations

> **"**
>
> *Jack Russells can and will find creative solutions to get out of yards, crates, front doors, etc. Before bringing one into your home, you should make certain that your fence is secure and that even the tiniest escape routes are secured. A climb-proof enclosure is also necessary for some JRTs. Indoors, they can and will take over your home, so it's necessary to have a training plan in place before bringing one home. Nothing is off-limits to a JRT—furniture, dining room tables, kitchen counters. It is important to set boundaries and have a safe and secure area for the dog both inside the home and outdoors so that it learns these boundaries. And be prepared to be challenged and stand your ground.*
>
> WENDY PALMER
> *Thistle Ridge Terriers*
>
> **"**

Check your fence line
- ▸ Check your fence line for any broken pieces, projecting nails, or holes. This is very important especially if your dog will have unsupervised time outside.

Address toxic plants in your yard
- ▸ Not all dogs will chew on plants, but puppies are especially prone to discovering their world through their mouths and may chew on potentially toxic plants. This can be prevented by fencing in plants so your dog doesn't have access to them or moving the plants to the front yard where your dog may not have unsupervised access to them.

In-ground pool fencing
- ▸ If your home has an in-ground pool, it is advisable to have a fence around it for many reasons, but especially so that your dog doesn't get into it unattended. Some dogs who love to swim can do it until they exhaust themselves to the point that they may not be able to get out.

Designated bathroom area

▸ This is not necessarily for safety but is something you may want to implement in your home to protect your lawn and also reduce the area you will have to clean up.

Outdoor product protection

▸ There are a lot of products used in backyards, gardens, and lawns that may be potentially hazardous to a dog. Fertilizers can have chemicals in them that may be toxic. Dogs can get sick eating the grease and drippings from your grill, and products kept in garages, like salt for melting ice, can be toxic. It is important to keep these products out of reach and/or to consider looking into dog-friendly alternatives. This is especially important for Jack Russell Terriers because they are known to be curious and may get into things that other dogs may not.

Regular costs of owning a dog

Trying to predict the cost of owning a dog is very hard because there are so many unforeseeable expenditures that may occur. However, there are routine costs that tend to be relatively consistent throughout the lifetime of your dog. It is advisable to place money aside each month for incidentals and any larger events that may come up in the future. The amount you may want to set aside is completely based on your personal means, but $100 a month is a very good start if you can manage it.

The yearly costs of owning a dog truly depend on your lifestyle and how much you spoil your dog. Some people love to buy clothes for their pets or other accessories and will spend more. People who choose the highest quality of dog food or who have a dog that needs a prescription diet will also end up spending more. Jack Russell Terriers are known to destroy toys, so you may end up buying more toys compared to other owners with different breeds.

The following breakdown will give you a general understanding of possible yearly costs for owning a dog:

BASIC COSTS OF OWNING A DOG

Photo Courtesy of Joann Bonafede

> ➢ **Food and Treats**

$300–$1200/year

> ➢ **Toys**

$10–$200/year

> ➢ **Beds**

$0–$100/year

> ➢ **Leashes and Collars**

$0–$100/year

> ➢ **Grooming**

$50–$200/year

> ➢ **Routine veterinary care**

$200–$800/year

> ➢ **Preventative medications and supplements**

$40–$200/year

> ➤ **Training classes or resources**
> ▸ $0–$500/year

> ➤ **Dog walking**
> ▸ $0–$2,000/year

> ➤ **Pet sitters or boarding**
> ▸ $0–$2,000/year

TOTAL: $600–$7,200

Pet insurance

Pet insurance has recently started to become more common. Currently, there are seven insurance companies that are the most widely available, each with different degrees of coverage. Pet insurance works slightly differently than human health insurance because the owner usually has to pay the cost up-front and then gets reimbursed.

The seven dominating insurance companies currently are ASPCA, Embrace, Figo, Nationwide, Petplan, Pets Best, and Trupanion.

When comparing pet insurance companies, there are some critical questions that should be considered.

What counts as a pre-existing condition? Do some chronic conditions become pre-existing when a new policy term begins?

This is a very important question to consider, especially if you are going to be adopting a dog. If you are getting a puppy, either by adoption or breeder, you will have fewer issues with pre-existing conditions if you get pet insurance from the beginning. If you decide to wait to get pet insurance and an event occurs before the coverage is effective, it may affect your coverage.

How is wellness, non-illness, or non-injury care covered?

This is also known as preventative care coverage. Some pet insurance includes this coverage. Some may work like a health savings plan, and in some insurance policies, preventative care is not covered.

Are veterinarians paid directly?

This is dependent on the plan and the veterinary clinic. When pet insurance first entered the marketplace, owners would usually pay the

full cost up-front and then file a claim for reimbursement, but that is starting to change.

Does the plan offer a trial period to pet owners?

Most plans offer a money-back guarantee 30 days after the plan
becomes effective.

Do plans use a benefit schedule?

Most plans do not offer a benefit schedule unless it comes to preventative care.

Are therapeutic diets covered?

Some insurance plans do cover therapeutic or prescribed diets, but it is
important to read the fine print here because a company may say it covers
a therapeutic diet, but it may only be for specific treatments such as bladder
stones or urinary crystals.

What dental work is covered? Are prophylaxes covered? If so, under what circumstances?

Most preventative dental work is not covered by insurance plans. A majority
of the plans only start covering dental work when there is a need to treat an
illness such as periodontal disease. Some only cover dental injuries or fractures.
This is important to consider because Jack Russell Terriers are prone to dental
disease and may require multiple dental procedures during their lifetime.

Are exam fees for accidents or illnesses covered?

With most of the pet insurance companies, exam fees for accidents or
illnesses are covered, which could save you upwards of $200 for a sick pet
exam, which is a significant amount that can be put toward treatment.

Are deductibles annual or per condition?

Almost all pet insurance companies have annual deductibles, but some
may have lifetime per- condition deductibles.

When are records required from the veterinary practice?

Some insurance may request medical records at the time of enrollment,
and this is just to assess if the pet has any pre-existing conditions. More
often than not, records will be requested directly from your veterinarian
after the first claim is submitted.

What are customer service hours and formats?

Most insurance companies keep business hours during the week and limited weekend hours, which can be challenging if you have an issue with your insurance during an emergency, especially during off-hours. If this is important to you, consider an insurance company that has 24/7 availability.

New dog shopping list

When bringing a new dog into your home, there are some items that you may want to have on hand in order to have a smooth transition. Some people like to buy these items ahead of time, while others like to bring their new dog with them to the store to let them choose. Either way, this list will provide a good base to start your new adventure with your pup.

SHOPPING LIST

Food

▸ If you are bringing a puppy home, it is advisable to start him out with puppy food because the ingredients are crafted for a puppy's growing body.

▸ If you are adopting an adult dog, it is advisable to discuss what the dog has been eating already and consult with your veterinarian as to what type of diet would be best for your dog.

Food and water bowls

▸ Food bowls are pretty simple. Stainless steel bowls or ceramic bowls are recommended because they don't retain bacteria like plastic bowls and are easier to clean.

▸ Water bowls should be a bit bigger than your dog's food bowl because dogs tend to drink more water throughout the day than they eat. Some people like the convenience of self-filling water bowls.

Treats

▸ Treats are a great way to positively reinforce good behaviors and should only be used when training. Some people make their own treats at home, which is a great alternative to store-bought ones.

Toys

▸ Toys are another great form of positive reinforcement, especially for Jack Russell Terriers, because it can feed that natural hunting drive. One of my favorite toys for my Jack Russell is a strip of fox fur. He goes nuts for it, and we only use it for hunting games in the house. Otherwise, he has a basket of toys that he gets on a day-to-day basis.

Bed

> Beds are great because not only are they a comfortable and soft space for your dog, but they also can reduce the amount of hair that ends up on your furniture. As mentioned before, I have a bed for my Jack Russell in almost every room of the house and one in my car.

Kennel or crate

> This is really important because it provides a safe space for your dog, and when he is trained correctly, it will let him be comfortable with a crate environment, which is important if he ever has to spend the night at a vet or a kennel. With Jack Russell terriers and their ability to squeeze out of small spaces, it might be advisable to get a metal crate compared to a soft or fabric crate.

Leash, collar, and/or harness

> Collars usually carry information and registration tags on them so your dog can be identified if he ever becomes separated from you. However, I recommend getting a harness, too, because Jack Russell Terriers do tend to pull on walks, especially if they get motivated by a bird or other animal and may choke themselves. A harness protects the dog's trachea and also can be used as a lifting apparatus if you ever need to pick him up in a hurry.

CHAPTER FOUR

Bringing Your Jack Russell Home

> "
>
> *The first few days and nights with any new puppy can be challenging. A Jack Russell will not quit until it wears itself out or you give in. Ideally, you should bring a JRT into your home when you have the time and flexibility to lose some sleep. Puppies will need to go out to eliminate every few hours, and nighttime is no exception. It's important to start establishing a routine immediately so the transition will go smoothly, and you can all settle into your new routine. I also recommend putting a small collar or harness on the new puppy, attaching a light lead to it, and keeping the puppy with you or in a secure area when you cannot watch it. If you are making the decisions for your new puppy, instead of letting him make all of the decisions, it makes setting boundaries and rules much easier during the acclimation process.*
>
> WENDY PALMER
> *Thistle Ridge Terriers*
>
> "

Managing expectations

This is one of the most important steps in training your Jack Russell. Setting expectations for yourself, your family, and your dog allows for an equal understanding of what behaviors are acceptable and which are not. If this is the first time you have had a dog, it is important to sit down and have a conversation on what rules will be applied to your new addition. When my boyfriend moved in, my Jack Russell had free access to the couch, slept in bed with me, and had a bed in almost every room and one for the car.

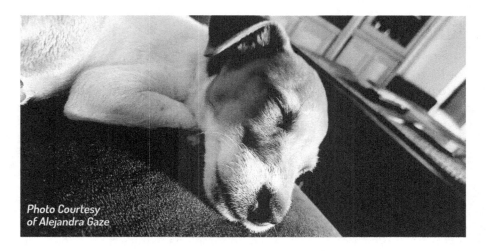

Photo Courtesy
of Alejandra Gaze

This was hard for my boyfriend. He had never had a dog before and did not like the idea of having a dog in bed or on the couch. However, Marty McFly had been a part of my home for nine years prior to my boyfriend's addition, so we had to manage his expectations. This was a point of contention for the first couple of months, but we made compromises and adjusted our expectations.

In order to start managing expectations, it is good to clarify what your expectations actually are. Start by writing down what you see when you think about your future with your dog. Do you dream of competing with your Jack Russell, cuddling on the couch, or exploring your local hiking trails? What is it going to take to get you and your dog to that point?

First, there are the standard expectations—not going to the bathroom in the house, not chewing on things that aren't dog friendly, etc. However, there are other expectations to consider, too, and these will change and evolve as you build a relationship with your dog. For example, do you want your dog to bark at the door when someone knocks or rings the doorbell? Do you want him to sleep in bed with you?

After you have taken your personal expectations into consideration, is there anyone else who gets a say? If you have roommates or a family, it is great to discuss expectations with them in order to make sure everyone is on the same page. For example, if you don't want your dog to have table scraps, everyone in the house needs to know that they can't give those things to your dog. If you don't want your Jack Russell on the furniture, good luck with that, but everyone needs to know. This will allow you to have consistent expectations across the board, which will be clearer to your dog. If the expectations are not consistent, your Jack Russell will use this to get his way.

42

Bringing your new dog home

The time has finally come, and you are going to pick up your new dog. In order to make sure the first ride home is a positive one, it is good to come into it prepared or even a little overprepared. First, consider how you are going to get your dog. This can range more than you think. Oftentimes, if you got your dog locally, there isn't much concern for logistics because you will most likely be driving. However, sometimes dogs or puppies are purchased or rescued from another state that may require a train or a flight in order to get them. By personal recommendation, I do not recommend ever flying a dog in the cargo of a plane. It is loud, scary, they don't know what is going on, and this can lead to a stressful transition into your new home.

If you are driving, bring a hard-sided or wire crate, toys, treats, chews, blankets and/or a bed, perhaps some puppy pads if it's a long road trip, bowls, water, and a collar or harness with a leash. It will be tempting to put your new dog in your lap and snuggle them the entire way home, but training and expectations start from the moment that paperwork is signed. If you are flying, check to see what airlines allow dogs in the cabin. Most will allow a Jack Russell-sized dog because they can fit under the seat in front of you. You will need an airplane-approved crate. I like using soft crates because they are flexible and usually have multiple access points to reach your new furry friend. And again, bring the above snack and provisions to encourage a comfortable ride. Note if you do bring a toy, try not to bring one with a squeaker because this may become annoying to your fellow passengers.

Make a plan for when you pick up your new dog. I always recommend picking up mid-morning because they should have already eaten and done their business before you have arrived, and it allows for you to take your time heading home. If you are driving, expect to make a few rest stops along the way so everyone can stretch their legs and go potty if needed. This is especially important if you are getting a young dog or puppy.

When you arrive home, it is important to introduce any other pets or family members slowly and not all crowd around your new addition because this can be severely overwhelming for them. Usually, I do this by starting in the fenced backyard, letting them sniff all the new smells, go potty if needed, and give them some time to explore their new environment. I often just sit and watch them as they explore and then encourage family members to do the same. Your dog will more than likely come to you and explore you some more, and this gives you the opportunity to talk sweet to them and give them some love or maybe even throw a toy. Once they start to relax, perhaps lay down, or hang around you more, I will introduce one of the other dogs.

*Photo Courtesy
of Katie Ward and Bob Hogan*

This can go a multitude of ways, but I had two well-behaved Border Collies when I added my little Marty McFly to the mix, so I didn't feel like I needed anyone on leash. Ideally, they would have already been introduced if you got an older dog, as we discussed earlier on. So this would be a reintroduction in a new environment. If you are unsure, I would put both dogs on leash and allow them to introduce themselves. If they seem excited and positive about the situation, ears perked and tails up and wagging, you can take one off-leash, see how they interact, and then take both off-leash. Keep them in the backyard, and allow them to desensitize themselves before you add another dog to the mix if you have one. Usually, I will introduce each dog individually and then allow them all to interact together once I feel confident that everyone is happy with the situation.

Eventually, once everyone is comfortable with one another, I will bring the dogs into the house. The same process should be considered for the house as was in the backyard. Everyone is now outside, so one person and your new dog go inside, allow for exploration, and then slowly add more people and dogs. If you have a cat or other pet that can't go outside, it would be best to do that interaction right after exploring the house before you add other people and dogs because it can become a little chaotic if there are multiple bodies moving around.

Once introductions are done, your normal routine can be continued to start building those schedules and expectations. The first day, and probably the first week, add some more cushion time to those routines because your dog is still learning and may need more assistance to understand the process.

The first week with your new family addition

> **"**
>
> *On the first night home, put the dog in a small crate (the same height as the bed) next to your bed. This way he won't have separation anxiety from leaving his littermates, and it will also help him learn that a crate is a safe place for him to feel secure. This ensures he can see you, but he is also in his own space and on the way to being crate trained. Take your JRT outside to potty just before bed. If he whines, just give the top of the crate a light tap to let him know you are there. If he wakes up in the middle of the night, take him out to potty and then come right back in and put him right back into the crate. This should not be fun time, eating time, etc. Usually, by the second or third night, JRTs get the routine.*
>
> DONNA MARIE
> *Celtic River Jacks*
>
> **"**

The first week really sets the foundation for the lifetime you are going to spend with your Jack Russell Terrier. Though dogs need a lifetime of training and structure, this first week is when he will test his boundaries. It might be helpful to take some time off during the first couple of days or first week you have your new Jack Russell. This allows you the time to monitor your Jack's behavior and lay the foundation of his training.

It is important that you stay as consistent as possible during the first week to solidify expectations and reduce misunderstandings. The first week it is also important to stick to a schedule so that your dog starts to understand routines. Having a Jack is going to add time to your normal routine. A walk in the morning, breakfast, and a potty break can easily add at least 30 minutes to an hour in the morning and again in the evening. This can be a significant change to your daily schedule, and having some time off to embrace this new schedule might help.

Choosing a veterinarian and the early vet visits

Choosing a veterinarian doesn't have to be challenging. Choosing a veterinarian includes a lot of the normal steps you take in assessing a new place to give your business, except this should also include a few extra steps because you are not just spending money there; you are entrusting a vet with the health of your pup.

Once you find a veterinarian and a veterinary clinic you like, see if you can schedule a visit without your pet. This will give you the chance to have a conversation with the staff. During this first assessment, you can ask what services they provide, if they are available after hours, or if your dog needs advanced diagnostics like an X-ray or ultrasound, whether they can do it there or if you'll have to go somewhere else.

Personal Recommendations

Personal recommendations go a long way when finding a vet because people who make recommendations will have had direct experience not only with the veterinarian themselves but the clinic and the staff. That said, personal recommendations should also be taken with a grain of salt in some sense because some visits to the veterinarian are very hard, and if that type of visit is the only one a person has had, they may only have negative opinions. Look for someone who has been going to a particular veterinarian for an extended period of time. They will have a greater understanding of the veterinarian and the type of medicine the clinic provides.

Does your veterinarian have experience with Jack Russell Terriers?

Now, this is not a requirement but more of a bonus point. Veterinarians will have experience with all sorts of breeds, but it is a huge bonus if they have additional experience with Jack Russell Terriers or they own one themselves. This is nice because the vet will then understand this particular breed and will tend to have more patience with them. Sometimes people have preconceived notions that Jack Russell Terriers will be hard to deal with without knowing the individual dog. It is good to have a veterinarian or staff that won't jump to conclusions based on breed.

FUN FACT
Royal Canines

Beth and Bluebell are a pair of Jack Russell Terriers adopted by Camilla, the Duchess of Cornwall. Beth was adopted at four months old in 2011, and Bluebell was adopted in 2012. The Terriers were adopted from the Battersea Dogs' Home in South London and can sometimes be seen accompanying the duchess around the city.

Licensed personnel or collective experience

Your veterinarian must have a degree in veterinary medicine and has to pass certain exams in order to practice, but this is not true for a clinic's technical staff. In a good practice, you will have at least a couple of licensed veterinary technicians (LVTs), registered veterinary technicians (RVTs), or certified veterinary technicians (CVTs). All these are the same; the title is just mandated by the state. These individuals have gone through a veterinary technician program and passed their final licensing exam.

Having licensed staff is only one factor to consider when selecting a veterinary clinic. Experience is really key in having a great veterinary team working on your dog. When looking into a veterinary practice, inquire about the collective experience as well as the individual experience of your prospective doctor and technicians.

The approach to medicine

When I moved to Colorado and started working at a specialty veterinary clinic, I was asked a question during my interview that has stayed with me. They asked, "Do you know how people consider their pets?" Of course, my reply was "like their children," but they corrected me. They said that pets are like an extension of people, and honestly, I believe it. This is something to consider when working with a clinic. Is their approach to medicine to see as many patients as possible a day to make a quota, or do they practice with the understanding that they are treating a member of your family or an extension of you?

Cost and Location

Diagnostics are always going to be expensive no matter where you go. However, some places tend to be more expensive because of the quality of staff or the advanced training a doctor may have. Location tends to be a bigger consideration, especially in an emergency. The closer your veterinarian is, the faster he or she can treat your dog in an emergency.

Comfort of your Jack Russell and yourself

My Jack Russell Terrier loves my veterinary clinic, and that means the world to me. Every time we come in, they call his name cheerily, and he is all over them in excitement. This relationship is important because it creates trust. This relationship takes time, but it is something you should be able to see when the clinic staff and doctors interact with clients and pets.

Once you have found a veterinary clinic and a veterinarian you like, it is time for the first set of vet visits. If you got a Jack Russell puppy, these vet visits will include vaccinations, deworming, starting on heartworm, flea and tick prevention, and a physical exam. It is important to make these visits as fun as possible by using positive reinforcement such as treats and praise to make visiting the veterinarian a good experience for your dog from the get-go.

Photo Courtesy of Lisa Mauro

Bonding with your Jack Russell

Every interaction you have with your Jack Russell is going to impact your relationship with him. Since Jack Russell Terriers are highly intelligent, driven, and a bit sassy, it is good to maintain a close but structured relationship with them. From day one, no aggressive behavior should be tolerated, and this includes behaviors that may seem cute or quirky such as mouthing your hands or protecting toys and food. We will discuss these specific behaviors later on, but they are important when starting to develop your bond.

The many forms of communication

There are many ways to communicate with your Jack Russell, including the tone of your voice, behavior, and body language. As an intelligent breed, they tend to clue into your emotions and any unconscious communication. When training and teaching your dog the rules of the house, a higher upbeat voice, usually paired with a slight rise of the shoulders whenever the dog does something good, tells him you are excited and happy with his behavior. On the other hand, a lower tone of voice and dropped shoulders indicates to the dog that he has done something wrong.

Once your dog learns the verbal cues associated with your body language, he can then learn what the terms mean. With Marty McFly, sometimes I come home and find something he had done, such as getting into the trash, for example. Often, he already knows he has done something wrong, but I can drop my shoulders and, in a low, slow tone, ask him, "Marty McFly, what is this?" and he knows that he did something inappropriate. After some training and time together, I can say, "Jack Russell!" which is my verbal cue when he was behaving in a negative way, such as if I could hear him getting into his dog food in the other room. I'll call out, and he will come bolting out with his ears down and tail tucked, knowing he is in trouble. When he does something good, I get really excited and break out into crazy playtime with a little wrestling and butt scratches, which for him is a high reward, thus deepening our bond because I am his ultimate reward for his positive behavior.

Start puppy training

Learning is an amazing way to start building a deep relationship with your Jack Russell. When training, it is important to use multiple forms of rewards, such as playtime with you directly, playing with a toy, and treats. This allows you flexibility in your reward system and the ability to keep your rewards fresh and interesting. When starting training, it is important to do short sessions throughout the day and at different locations. This allows you to teach your dog that you expect that behavior in all types of environments,

*Photo Courtesy
of Nina Chang and Brooke Lloyd*

not just at home without distractions. This also allows you to solidify your communication and commands so your Jack Russell can understand what you are asking him to do.

Structured play

Structured play combines training and play together. Does your puppy want that super-exciting stuffed rabbit toy? Great; he just has to sit first for it. Then he will get rewarded with high-intensity play after. There are a lot of games you can play with your dog that will reinforce his training while being exciting and entertaining. Jack Russell Terriers can get very excited, and accidents can occur, such as a bite to your hand instead of the toy. Those are training moments for you and your dog equally. If something like this occurs, make sure to stop the play, correct the behavior, and then continue on. Don't just accept it because the dog got excited. What if he gets excited at the dog park and accidentally bites someone else? Structured play makes you responsible for controlling the limits of what is acceptable dog behavior and what is not.

Quiet time

For high-drive dogs with exponential energy, you may have to train them on when to turn off and relax. For Marty McFly, this comes in a few different forms. Usually, I use the command, "That will do," which cues him to stop what we are doing. I most often use this if we are playing tug-of-war or when I come home from work.

When I first came home from work, Marty Mcfly used to jump all over me and bark, which was something I did not like. We worked on this by first teaching him to go grab me a toy when I came home to prevent him from barking, and then I made sure I stayed neutral in my tone and body language and used the verbal cue "that will do" to stop him from jumping. If he was excessively happy, I would command him to go to bed. That is our time-out zone, which means he needs to go calm down. When I saw he was settled enough, I released him, and then we had a few minutes of bonding time, playing with the toy he was still holding and giving him heavy pets. This system may be different for you and your Jack Russell, but it is important for him to learn how to turn off in order to create a good balance in your life and training.

Building tolerance and patience

This is one of the most important parts of training and bonding with your Jack Russell because it also builds trust between the two of you. Developing a tolerance tends to go hand in hand with asserting your control in the most neutral way possible. Often how I start to build this is by placing my puppy on his back while he's in my lap. This innately is a submissive position for dogs, and Jack Russell Terriers particularly don't like to be put on their backs. I hold a puppy there with gentle control until he settles. As soon as he relaxes, I reward him by releasing him. This is so important because it allows a dog to learn tolerance and patience as well as reminding him who is in control. Down the line, when he needs to get procedures done at the vet or have his toenails clipped, he will already be comfortable with restraint and will be more apt to tolerate whatever procedure is required.

Bonding is going to take time, and it is something that is strengthened every day based on your interactions with your dog. The more consistent you are, the better he will behave and learn. The more time you spend with your dog, the stronger this relationship will be.

CHAPTER FIVE
Building the Foundation

> "
>
> *After spending 25 years training Jack Russells professionally, I always tell people that they learn very fast. The challenge is getting them to use what you teach them! Jack Russells are fierce and independent and are bred to be that way to do the job they were created for. If you don't find something that is of high value to them, they will typically move on to something else. They can be taught to do almost any command or any job. Your job is to make sure you make it worth their while! A certain amount of leadership combined with partnership is the key to successfully training your Terrier. You must be firm and clear in communicating and teaching him what you expect, but you also need to make certain he knows that when he does what you are asking of him, he will be rewarded in a way that makes it worth his effort. It is a delicate balance but one that can be easily achieved when you keep the dog's intelligence in mind.*
>
> WENDY PALMER
> *Ridge Terriers*
>
> "

Standing by your expectations

We have discussed multiple times the importance of setting expectations for your dog. Standing by these expectations and making sure you stay consistent will lead to a well-behaved dog and companion. However, it is also important to assess your standards. If you find your dog is having difficulties achieving these expectations, it is good to make sure these expectations are realistic. Your dog is an individual and will have preferences. For example, Marty McFly was never a fan of any tricks that involved his paws, but he loved learning tricks that involved him spinning or jumping. I adapted my expectations to his abilities. Once those expectations were modified to his abilities, I made sure to maintain those new standards.

Photo Courtesy
of Nina Chang and Brooke Lloyd

Training yourself and your family

> *Jack Russells are experts at training people. I tell new owners the rule of three... the first time anything happens, it is a surprise. The second time, it is learned. By the third time the same action is repeated, it is now a habit. If it was a positive action, yeah! Come, sit, stay, look down...BUT, if it was a bad habit, barking, digging, biting, chasing, etc., now you have to break a habit, and that can seem impossible. The best punishment for a Jack Russell is to IGNORE the dog. As soon as the bad behavior passes, immediately reward and interact. An excellent way to interact when training a Jack Russell is the Dr. Jekyll / Mr. Hyde method. Set aside specific times for structured training. Use simple commands with little emotion. Make each session 10–30 minutes long, and then put the puppy in his safe space afterward for 5–10 minutes to 'think' about what he just did. When you return to the dog, be his best, most loving friend... lots of hugs and cuddles, and fun play. You will be amazed by how quickly your dog learns the skills and applies them when you are being his loving human. You can teach him to come up and down with your body language and simple rules.*
>
> SUE ANNE WILSON
> *West Elk Terriers*

Setting these expectations for your dog is a wonderful place to start, but it is wise to make sure that these expectations are shared with all other people in your home. This is important to maintain your dog's expectations no matter who the person is, so the dog will be well-behaved no matter who is asking him to perform a behavior. This is probably going to be the hardest aspect of training your Jack Russell. As we know, they are a brilliant breed that will find any and all weaknesses. Your dog will see who in your home will bend the rules and let him get away with whatever he wants.

When Marty McFly wants to get away with getting on the bed and cuddling or getting some scraps of food, he knows to come to me. I know, I am the worst. But when he wants to get away with other things, like if he is bored in the house and wants to go for a walk, he knows to go to my fiancé. My fiancé would walk him twenty times a day if Marty McFly felt so inclined.

When I lived with roommates, Marty McFly would get away with not having to sit or do work for treats and gained a lot of weight because they just gave him food whenever he wanted.

It is not only for maintaining behavior that we strive to maintain these standards. It can also be directly correlated to maintaining your dog's health. Jack Russell Terriers have a lot of energy, but that doesn't mean they can't be overfed, which can lead to obesity. If someone riles your dog up often, allows him to play-bite, and encourages rough play in general, this can lead to an accidental bite that goes too deep. These are just some examples of why it is good to make sure that everyone in your home is on the same page in terms of expectations for your dog and themselves.

Photo Courtesy of Emma Walker

Creating a safe space in a crate

> *The puppy will likely cry/whimper in the crate. Do not pamper your new baby, or you set the stage for its entire life. Remember to set the rules that will apply to the puppy for the rest of its adult life.*
>
> N. GAYE REDPATH-SCHAEPER
> *Conquest Terriers*

Dogs are innately den animals, and the crate acts like a domesticated version of the dens their ancestors once inhabited. This space is the only part of the house that is solely your dog's and should be only a positive and safe space for him. This environment should be comfy, with plenty of padding and blankets, toys, and even a bowl for water. The crate should be big enough that your dog can stretch out comfortably but not so big that he has a potty area. Dogs treat this den space as if it is their own bedroom and will instinctively want to keep it clean and not soil it. This is a great benefit for using a crate to help with housebreaking.

Your dog's crate is the one place in the home where he can do no wrong. Your voice and body language should never be negative or aggressive toward your dog while he is in there, and the crate should not be used as a place of punishment. The crate should always be open and available for your dog, so whenever he needs a safe place, he can go there. Often when something scary occurs, like fireworks or friends yelling suddenly at a score in a football game, Marty McFly will run to his kennel for safety. The more he has aged, the less he runs to his crate, but I still like to keep it available just in case.

Having the kennel constantly available also allows you to use it quickly if needed. All my dogs have been trained to go into their crate by verbal command. I personally use "kennel up," and they will instantly stop what they are doing and go into their kennels, waiting for me to come and close them in. This verbal command has been useful when I have dropped a Pyrex pan that shattered across the kitchen and into the living room. I simply told Marty McFly to "kennel up" so he could be in a safe space while I cleaned up the dangerous mess.

Chewing

Chewing is a natural behavior in dogs. A dog's mouth has essentially the same purpose that human hands have. When humans are young, we interact and discover our world by picking things up and inquiring about them. We ourselves have a stage in which we put everything in our mouths as a secondary form of inquiry. Dogs also explore the world by sniffing things and then putting them in their mouths.

Dogs also chew because it is a natural way for them to maintain their jaw muscles, and it helps keep their teeth clean. This is an ancestral behavior that once allowed wolves to hunt down and tear into prey. Domesticated dogs no longer have to do this, so they often need an outlet for this primal-rooted behavior. If an outlet is not given to them, they will find one.

The first step in addressing chewing is to give your dog a set of chew-friendly objects. The second is to educate him on what is okay to chew on and what is not. This step, especially with puppies, will take time and sometimes repetitive correction. Again, your puppy is discovering what he can chew on and is going to have to look to you for guidance. Some of my favorite chews for puppies and dogs include Nylabones and natural antlers. I find these types of chews cue into that primal urge.

When you discover your pup chewing on something he shouldn't, correct him immediately with a quick no or "uh ah," and then immediately follow up with something that is okay to chew on. This will have to be repeated multiple times, and again, dogs are individuals who may have different preferences. If your dog isn't interested in the antlers or Nylabone and is constantly chewing on the cushion of your couch, he may prefer softer toys to chew on. Correct the couch chewing with a stuffed toy instead.

Marty McFly loves both hard chews and soft toys. He has one soft toy that he has had for years that he loves and even knows the name of it. All other soft stuffed toys he makes sure to rip open and tear out their guts, leaving little bits of fluff all over the house

FAMOUS JRT's
Wishbone

Wishbone was a popular children's television show that aired on PBS in the 1990s. The show's star was a Jack Russell Terrier named Wishbone who reenacted classical works of literature in period costume to teach a lesson or solve a problem faced by his owner, Joe Talbot. Wishbone was referred to as a "little dog with a big imagination." *Wishbone* won several awards, including four Daytime Emmys and a Peabody award.

and attached to his tiny teeth. Again, a natural behavior that we have given an approved outlet for.

Now, in some scenarios, your dog knows what he is allowed to chew on and what he is not, but then one day, he may still decide to chew and destroy something at random. This can be an indication of a lot of things and will leave you trying to figure out what's going on. Some dogs, especially older ones, may have an underlying health issue, or they may have started new meds that are causing them to be hungry, so he is chewing to satiate that hunger. Or, if your dog is not properly crate trained, or he finds himself in a crate too long, he may start chewing at the crate because he wants out. Chewing on an object at random can also mean a dog is stressed, and this usually occurs when you have left him alone for extended periods of time. Dogs communicate this stress and frustration with you by destroying or chewing on something unusual, such as a pair of shoes that you've owned forever or a cover of a book that you are currently reading.

In these scenarios, I advise stepping back and seeing what changed in your routine that could have provoked this new behavior. Did you have to run errands after work that extended the amount of time you left your dog alone at home? Have you been busier at work, so you haven't been able to exercise your dog as much? More often than not, a new destructive behavior is a reaction to a routine change or a decrease in something your dog may need. Often Jack Russell Terriers will develop destructive behaviors because they are not getting enough attention or exercise.

Growling and aggression

Jack Russell Terriers were bred to be hunting dogs, so they naturally have an aggressive nature and growl and bark often. Because of this, many people misconstrue these behaviors as bad habits that are uncontrollable and give Jack Russells up at a very young age. I have found using this natural behavior and shaping it into play, exercise, and entertainment makes Marty McFly happy and docile. In addition, I had to maintain strict expectations for Marty McFly from early on and let him know constantly that he would not be able to get away with any aggressive growling, nipping, or biting.

Growling, in the language of dogs, can have a lot of connotations to it and is really on a very wide spectrum. There is growling in play, growling in fear, growling in warning, and everything in between. It is important to understand what your dog is trying to tell you with his growl and react accordingly.

When playing tug-of-war with your dog, you will probably notice he will growl, and this is usually in play. In fact, Marty McFly will grab his favorite tug and bring it to me, play bow with it in his mouth, and start growling. This is him enticing me to play and is something that dogs often do to one another to encourage playful interaction.

Often when Marty McFly and I go to the dog park, there is one goofy, long-legged giant, who doesn't know if Marty is a dog, cat, or very interesting play toy, and he will come up and hit him with his paw as if to poke him. Marty McFly

Photo Courtesy of Miranda Reddish

hates this with a passion and will puff himself up, drop his tail, lower his ears, and growl. This is him warning the other dog that he wants the other dog to stop before he loses his temper. More often than not, the dog doesn't take these warnings seriously, continues the behavior, and then Marty will explode, snapping and jumping up against him. This usually leads to the owner of the other dog getting very upset. I then have to educate the person on dog behavior and on how my dog is not at fault.

This scenario is also why I am not fond of dog parks, especially when they are busy because people aren't paying attention to their dogs and only see the outcome from a buildup.

Growling is a form of communication. As well as nipping and biting, this is how puppies learn boundaries from other dogs. The dog who keeps on pushing Marty did not have this education at a young age, so he never learned these boundaries. Puppies will use these same behaviors with humans to assess these boundaries. When a puppy nips or bites at you and he is not corrected, you are not letting him know what boundary he is crossing and are allowing him to believe that this is acceptable behavior.

There are two ways I addressed nipping and biting with Marty when he was young. First, when he got all worked up or took it too far, I gave him a time-out. I did this by telling him, "that's enough," picking him up, and placing him on his back in my lap. I would not release him until he stopped trying to nip and relaxed. While waiting, I would repeat "settle" in a calm, lowered voice until he eventually relaxed. As soon as he stopped and relaxed, I would say "good settle" and then release him.

When your dog is young, this may take some time and patience, but do not give up! We have been so consistent on this all of McFly's life that I can now tell him "Enough" in the middle of play, and he will stop what he is doing immediately and settle down. Jack Russell Terriers need an off switch, and this is what worked best with me.

Secondly, every time McFly nipped or bit me when he was a puppy, I would say, "OW!" and then put my hand over his nose and press his lip against the tips of his teeth so if he decided to bite down again, he would be biting himself and not me. This is a technique that mothers often use on young pups to put them in their place, but instead of a hand, they will place their mouths over their pups' muzzles.

Barking

Jack Russell Terriers are bred to bark; that is just a part of their natural behavior, and it is something that can be addressed but will be a lifelong training issue. For Marty McFly and me, our means of addressing this is by redirection, and so far, it has been very successful. However, he does have a bit of separation anxiety, and if I leave him in a crate all day, he will bark his little head off. When I am home and McFly barks excessively, I will usually say, "Hey, that's enough," and then tell him to go get a toy or toss a ball for him, and that does the trick. The barking in the kennel when I am gone is a challenge we have been working with for a long time and continue to work with to this day.

I did not kennel train McFly correctly to begin with. I know this, and man, am I paying the price for it. He never had to be alone for the first five years of his life, and then one day, I got a job where he couldn't come to work with me anymore, and everything changed. I tried kenneling him at first, and he would dig at the crate and bark nonstop. Even if I placed treats, frozen Kongs, or all his favorite toys in there, he was just pissed off that I had left him. Now we have come up with a compromise in which he has a whole room to himself that he can stay in while I am gone, and he is much better. I do not give him the run of the house because he has been known to act out. So, he has a room where he has multiple beds, toys, a water bowl, and a chair so he can look out the front window and watch for me to come home.

For some people, it is helpful to have a doggie nanny cam up to get alerts about when their dogs are barking at home, so they can tell them to stop over a speaker. These do help with a lot of dogs and allow you to see what your dog does when he is at home alone. However, not all jobs allow you to have your phone on you, or you may not be available to react immediately as soon as you get an alert, which can defeat the purpose.

For some people, it is helpful to have a dog walker come once a day to take them on a walk, which allows them to get some exercise and have a potty break. This can be super beneficial if you make it a part of your normal routine. For McFly, however, we didn't start this until later in life, and he developed more anxiety and destructive behavior when the dog walker came because he then had to experience someone leaving him not just once but twice in a day, which was very frustrating for him.

Separation anxiety

Most of the behavior I have been discussing in Marty McFly can be defined as separation anxiety. This is directly correlated to the fact that I never taught him at a young age how to be alone. He now hates to be in a crate, will sometimes pee in the house, and will bark all day long if he is in a small, confined place. He honestly has spoiled dog syndrome, which we have seen in a lot of dogs that became part of a home during the pandemic. These dogs have become used to being close to their owners and get highly anxious when their people are no longer close by. Dogs are innately social animals and form strong attachments to other dogs and people. Jack Russell Terriers often grow these strong attachments with their owners.

The first time puppies deal with separation anxiety is when they are separated from their mother and littermates, which often leaves them restless for their first few nights in their new home. During this time, you become the puppy's new social attachment. This is why it is important to create a routine that includes time away from your dog at a very early age.

In addition to implementing these periods of alone time, it is also important to make sure that you make your coming and going drama-free. Don't give your dog long goodbyes when you leave, and don't make coming home exciting. Making your leaving and returning uneventful will prevent your dog from thinking that your leaving and returning are a big deal. The less of an event it is, the less likely your dog will develop separation anxiety.

Separation anxiety can be exhibited by your dog in the form of chewing, digging, licking, pacing, urinating or defecating in the house, and vomiting. Sometimes dogs may mouth at your shoes or nip and growl when you are leaving. They are not doing these things to get even or to seek revenge; they are doing them to reduce their tension. They love you so much and want to be with you so badly that it makes them anxious when you leave. There are a variety of things you can do to prevent this anxiety.

Tips for Preventing Separation Anxiety

- Increasing exercise can help reduce this anxiety. It is good to create both mental and physical exercise routines for your dog daily. A good walk in the morning followed by ten minutes of trick training and again in the evening will help maintain your dog's need for energy expenditure.

- Give your dog a toy that he has to work to get treats from. This can be as simple as treats frozen in broth that you put in the dog bowl, a Kong filled with peanut butter, or a puzzle toy that your dog has to dig at or toss in order to get treats. These types of chews and toys will occupy your dog's mind and let him forget about you leaving. Usually, I will give Fly his frozen treat 10 minutes before I plan to leave so that he can be completely preoccupied while I slip out the door. I will also place his puzzle toy down right before I leave so he can go to something else if he finishes his frozen treat quickly.

- In general, you should ignore your dog for 15–20 minutes before you leave and also for about 20 minutes after you return home to make these moments feel less like events and just part of your family's normal routine.

- Your dog will also pay attention to what you do prior to leaving for a short amount of time compared to a long amount of time. If I am just running to the store, I may grab just my wallet, put on my flip-flops, and a couple of bags. If I am going to work, I will do the above, but also make my coffee, maybe put on different types of shoes, grab my car keys, etc. Try to mix up these clues so your dog can't associate a specific behavior with you and the length of time you will be gone. For example, do everything you would do to go to work and then come back ten minutes later.

- Worst-case scenario, if you have tried everything you can but your dog's anxiety hasn't lessened, speak to your veterinarian for prescription or supplement assistance that you can use in conjunction with your training. Some veterinarians are seeing benefits with CBD and separation anxiety. Your vet may have other suggestions that could also help with your specific situation.

Building a solid recall

Recall is a term we use that refers to your dog stopping whatever he is doing and coming back to you directly when his name is called, and/or you use a verbal command like "come." Having a solid recall is one of the most beneficial commands your dog can learn because it allows you to protect him from danger, brings him back to you when he's off-leash and gives you more control. Some books do not recommend taking your Jack Russell off-leash for the first year or two of his life because he may get enticed by some sort of prey and take off with a slim possibility he will return. This is because Jack Russells have such high prey drives and were bred to never back down from chasing their quarry. Part of me agrees with this, but part of me also believes that if you train a solid recall, you can adventure with your Jack Russell, even off-leash.

For the first year of Marty McFly's life, I did keep him on a leash. When he developed a decent recall, I eventually used a thin, long cord, like a lunge line, attached to his leash and took him to fields, on trails, and in the woods to practice his recall from a greater distance. Now, with Marty McFly as an adult, I can have him off-leash and have confidence that I could call him back to me if needed. That being said, there are two scenarios in which I know that his recall ability goes right down the drain. If there is a fight at the dog park, he will dart right for it and get involved with no concept of my existence. It is not that he wants to be aggressive, but more he is trying to act like the fun police and break up the fight.

Secondly—and this has only happened once, but I thought for sure he was gone—we were in the backcountry in a field when he was sniffing at a bush, and two snow doves came swooping out of it right in front of his nose. He took off after them like it was the last thing he was going to do, and a part of me was worried that I might never see my dog again. I panicked for a solid minute, then stopped calling him, stood where I had last left him, and waited. It was about ten to fifteen minutes later that I saw him coming back down the trail, worried that he had also lost me. In that type of situation, completely unpredictable and uncontrollable, I kicked myself for not having him on leash, but his hunting instinct brought him back to me.

When I was teaching Marty McFly to sit, I began the foundation of his recall training. I would make him sit, tell him to stay, take a step back, and then release him to me. This had a twofold effect: it allowed me to teach him to wait or stay and also to come to me because I would have his reward. I would eventually build this up by taking two steps back, then three, then four, so on and so forth. Then I would start from the beginning again, but this time with distractions.

I started with toys on the floor. Then we would add higher distractions like treats and even other dogs. Once I felt pretty solid at home with this, I would do this on walks and go to different public places when there were all sorts of distractions around us. Up until this point, Marty McFly would be on leash, so I would still have control in case he did get distracted. Once I became confident with his abilities on leash, I went back to the basics, but this time without the support of the leash.

When you go back to basics and take the leash away, expect your dog to be more tempted by distractions. I will only ever give Marty three attempts maximum to heed my command. If your dog is thoroughly distracted when you try to call him, turn away and run. This makes you the most exciting thing that is happening at that moment. When he catches up with you, reward him greatly for his return and then take a break. Often dogs start becoming distracted during training sessions because they are stressed, bored, or tired. This is your dog letting you know that he has reached his maximum learning ability for the day.

You are not going to develop this recall in a day, a week, or a month. Like all things, this is something that has to be constantly refreshed and worked on. To encourage his connection to return to me, I love playing hide-and-seek with Marty McFly in the house. When he is distracted, sleeping, or sunbathing, I will try to sneak away and hide and then call him to find me. He loves this game because it allows him to use his hunting instincts, but also it teaches him that finding me is the greatest reward because once he finds me, we get to play, and he gets all the attention he could ever want.

Be creative in the ways you solidify your dog's recall. When you are out for a walk, let him wander ahead on leash and get distracted by the smells, and then call him back to you. Go to the dog park when it's empty, and let him wander away, and then call him to you. If he doesn't come, turn and run away as fast as you can to get him to enjoy the game. When I am reinforcing this recall, I not only play with McFly, but he gets some of his favorite treats and toys too. It makes coming back to me the best part of the adventure for him, and I want to keep it that way.

Creating a routine

Routines and training go hand in hand. Our educational systems have schedules and routines because it fosters stability, which allows for learning and growth to occur. In this book, we talk a lot about how developing a routine will also help make clear expectations for both you and your dog. From the very beginning, when McFly came home as a puppy, I tried to develop a standard routine that he could rely on. When we get up, we go outside to go potty. Then I get dressed and put my shoes on to take him for a walk. Once we are back, he gets breakfast as I prepare for work, and then he goes into his room when I am gone. Once I come home, he goes right outside to go potty, we play, we go for a walk, and then we start our evening routine. He can rely on this, and part of me can too.

It is, however, important to also deviate from routines in case unexpected things occur and to allow your dog to learn to become adaptable. Take your dog camping one weekend and see how he does. Allow your dog to stay at a friend's house (did someone say puppy sleepover?) so he can live with someone else's routine. By providing more experiences and slight diversions to routine, your dog will be able to handle separation better, and this will also help him adapt to unexpected timelines.

If your routine is too stringent, you may start to see behaviors that are associated with it. For example, you may see anxiety build up if you are late coming home from work one day, or the excitement leading up to dinnertime may lead your dog to become pushy or demanding. These diversions do not have to be extreme by any means; they can be small, like going right instead of left on your daily walk, visiting the beach instead of the dog park, or varying the amount of time you are gone from home. Of course, these don't have to be done every day of the week, but once a week or a couple of times a month can help your dog become more flexible.

CHAPTER SIX
Housebreaking

Expectations

> "
>
> *As with all puppies, remember to take it slowly, and remember that the best defense is a good offense. Anticipate when the pup will need to go—after sleeping, after playing, after eating—and get him outside before he needs to go. Praise, praise, and more praise when he 'performs'!*
>
> PATTI STORMS
> *Rabble Rouser Jack Russell Terriers*
>
> "

Housebreaking, in theory, is a relatively simple concept, and ideally, it means that your puppy will be trained to not go to the bathroom in the house and will only go potty outside. It seems simple enough. However, this can be a challenging concept to get across, especially based on the puppy or rescue dog's personal background and any other dogs in the house, as well as how consistent your training is.

For the full disclosure, Marty McFly is only 98% house-trained, and that is 100% my fault. He knows that he is not supposed to go to the bathroom in the house, he knows how to alert me when he has to go outside, and he knows where specifically outside he can and should go to the bathroom. However, he does have this little stubborn behavior that I like to call "spite peeing," and sometimes, he also "spite poops."

The reason I say this is 100% my fault is because, at the end of the day, it is. When I first got Marty McFly, and for the first eight years of his life, I worked in veterinary medicine. He really didn't have to be crate trained because he always came to work with me. He would hang out in a bed in the treatment room or was in a kennel/run with his other dog friends. I could let

him out whenever. Now, however, I have to go to a job, so being locked up in a crate, or even a room of my apartment, is a total disaster in his mind, and his retaliation is to pee. So, you see, it was my fault for not giving him the proper training from the beginning.

I know you are probably curious about the spite pooping. It only happened once, but I will remember it to my dying day. The first time we visited my mother's house, Marty was only about one or two years old. The first day, he jumped up on my mother's lap, and she petted him. The second day, however, he jumped up, and she pushed him off. He took note of this and sometime in the night pooped on the floor on her side of the bed, so she stepped in that warm pile first thing in the morning. I think this was completely intentional and spiteful on his part. Because he has never done it again, and especially has never done it to me. It leads me to believe he was hurt by her not accepting him, and he let her know about it!

The important lesson to take away from these stories is that expectations both on your side and your dog's need to be clarified and managed appropriately. Are your expectations simply that you don't want your dog to go to the bathroom inside or that you want him to use a special part of the yard? Do you want him to go to the bathroom mostly when he is on a walk, or do you want him to go potty before your walk so that you don't have to carry poop around in a bag? Take a few minutes to envision what potty expectations are for your dog, write them down, and stick to them. Consistency is key!

Techniques

There is essentially the same outcome that is wanted no matter what housebreaking technique you use. Your dog realizes he needs to use the bathroom; he alerts you; you let him outside; he goes potty—end of story. The biggest training aspect is the transition from your dog realizing he needs to go potty to alerting you. This alerting behavior can look different depending on what you want your dog to do.

Marty and I have the understanding that when he realizes he has to go potty, he will get up and go to the door. However, if I am distracted, he has expanded this alert to coming to find me, wagging his tail excitedly, and then running to the door. If I do not follow him, he will come back in the same fashion but also bounce off my leg gently to get my undivided attention and let me know that this is not a drill. Then, eventually, I get the urgency and let him out into the backyard. It is important to realize that there is training done on both sides: I have trained him to let me know, but he has also trained me to respond to him and his alerting me of his need to go potty.

The very beginning of house-training, outside of creating expectations, is to develop a routine. Puppies should be fed three times a day. An adult dog should be fed twice a day unless otherwise directed by your veterinarian. Puppies usually take six hours to digest food and will then have to go potty. Plan your schedule accordingly, and be prepared for some late-night walks if needed. It is good practice to allow your puppy to eat and then take him outside because eating can trigger him to go potty, and this will be a great opportunity for scheduled training.

Our routine usually looks something like this. In the morning, I get up and dressed and take Marty out for a potty and a walk. Then I feed him, take a shower, do my personal morning routine of getting ready for work, and then I let him out into the backyard one more time for any last-minute potty needs before I leave for work. Essentially the same routine happens in the evening in

HISTORICAL FACT
Polar Opposites

British explorer Sir Ranulph Fiennes and his wife Ginny owned a Jack Russell Terrier named Bothie. When Fiennes and his wife undertook their three-year transglobal expedition, they brought then two-year-old Bothie along with them, making him the first dog to have set paws on both the North and South Poles. The journey took place between 1979 and 1982, and Bothie was named "Pet of the Year" by England's Kennel Club upon his return.

reverse order. When I come home, I let him into the backyard to potty, then feed him, and do my evening routines. Once I have finished dinner and dishes, I take him for a long walk in the evening. Puppies, however, need a food and potty break usually halfway through the day to help them gain more understanding of the routine.

One of the best housebreaking methods is using a crate. As we discussed earlier, the crate is like your dog's bedroom, and he usually wants to maintain a clean environment. This natural instinct helps with housebreaking.

When it is time to feed your puppy, place his food in his crate, and let him eat in there with the door closed. Make sure you are paying attention because once he

Photo Courtesy of Susan DeWeese

is done eating and starts to feel the urge to go potty, he will probably start whining and may scratch at the crate door. This is when I introduce the question, "Do you want to go potty?" Once the dog shows me this behavior, I will ask that question, then take him out of the crate and go right outside. For the first couple of days, you may want to carry him, so he doesn't go immediately in the house.

Once the dog is outside and in the area I want him to go potty, I give the command, "go potty." Once he pees or poops, I make sure to praise him while saying, "good go potty!" and making this a very strong positive reinforcement. Staying consistent with this routine and these commands will really open the communication lines between you and your dog and lead to a good housebreaking experience.

Using puppy pads or paper training has gone in and out of vogue. More often than not, I find puppies tend to just tear up the puppy pads instead of using them as they were intended. For Jack Russell Terriers, I do not recommend puppy pads because they are too clever and are more inclined to bend the rules and will end up peeing on the bookshelf near the puppy pad or using the puppy pad to cover where they chose to pee or poop instead.

Positive reinforcement

Crates and attentiveness are going to be key in housebreaking your Jack Russell, and trust me—this may take time and patience. The most important part is to stay positive and always praise your puppy every time he goes potty outside. Jack Russell Terriers are very responsive to positive reinforcement and want to please you.

Even when accidents do happen in the house, it is something that can be corrected with a solid and strong, "NO!" immediately followed by some sort of command that refers to going outside. I use "Let's go outside" as my command, and then I make sure to take the dog to the usual potty spot that I use regularly. Once he goes potty in the appropriate area, make sure you

Photo Courtesy
of Katie Egerton

reinforce this behavior with positivity, a small treat, and praise. Sticking your dog's nose into his mess is not going to make this experience any easier or make him learn any faster. In fact, it can be detrimental to his learning.

Going to the restroom in the house, especially at a young age, is usually due to a lack of knowledge of where it is acceptable to go potty. Adult dogs, especially rescues, may just not know better. If you end up having a dog that was previously house-trained and has started to have accidents in the house, this may be a sign that something medical is going on. Make sure to check with your veterinarian. This may require bloodwork, a urine check, or another type of check-up.

Staying consistent

"

Consistency! Crate train your puppy from the beginning so that he always has a safe place to go. Make certain to set schedules for feeding and also monitor water intake so you can keep track of when he will need to go out and eliminate. Keep the puppy attached to you with a small collar or harness attached to a light leash so that he cannot sneak off and potty. Don't correct a puppy after he potties in the house—you will just teach him to be sneakier about where he goes. If you make a mistake, and he does go in the house in an area that is not appropriate, clean it up with an odor-eliminating product and start over and do better the next time. Puppies cannot be allowed to make decisions on their own for a while, so it is your responsibility to set them up for success. When taking your puppy outside, take him to one area and reward him after he potties outside. If your puppy is being stubborn or doesn't need to eliminate, make certain not to take him back inside and give him the freedom to go. I will put a dog in his crate for 10 or 15 minutes and then try again and repeat the process of taking him out and back in until the desired result is achieved. Patience, consistency, and perseverance are the keys to a successful potty-training experience.

WENDY PALMER
Thistle Ridge Terriers

"

*Photo Courtesy
of Nina Chang and Brooke Lloyd*

Consistency is key to owning and training a Jack Russell. I know I've said this over and over again, but it is the most important aspect of training. Sticking to a schedule is key, especially at a young age. Once your puppy gets accustomed to the schedule and has gone months without an accident in the house, it may be okay to start making modifications. When modifications to the schedule begin, make sure just to make small changes and be attentive to how your dog reacts. If accidents begin again, maybe the change was too soon or too significant, and you may have to adjust back. This process is all about flexibility and having a good relationship with your dog so you both can communicate your needs to one another.

Photo Courtesy of Whitney Adams

Here are some key things to remember about housebreaking and staying consistent with your puppy or newly rescued dog:

- Always take your dog outside after feeding.

- Make sure you give your puppy the opportunity to go potty first thing in the morning and last thing before going to bed.

- Allow your puppy the opportunity to go outside often throughout the day.

- Make sure to be consistent with the location in which you take your dog to go potty. These familiar smells will encourage him to go potty in the same area.

- Praise, praise, praise your puppy when he properly goes potty outside!!!

- Pay attention to how he is alerting you of his need to go potty.

- Make sure everyone is on the same page in your household, so there is consistency with commands, potty locations, and potty times.

CHAPTER SEVEN
Socialization is Key

> *Socializing is the single most important thing when raising any kind of puppy. Start by socializing from a distance and then move forward with one-on-one introductions as the puppy and other dogs show signs of being comfortable and ready to be introduced to one another. Another great way to do this is by using a barrier first. Put the puppy in an exercise pen and let the other dog free outside of it. This way, the dogs can safely introduce themselves through the barrier, and everyone involved will feel comfortable with it.*
>
> STEPHANIE PEDERSEN
> *Connemara Terriers*

Little dog, big personality

Jack Russell Terriers are basically the definition of the Napoleon Complex, believing they are bigger than they actually are. They have big personalities, and they are not afraid to use them on man or beast. This is why it is so important to begin socialization and training early on in your relationship. It sets the bar for what is appropriate and what is not. You are the one who must be the dominant member of the household; otherwise, your Jack Russell will push the boundaries and assert himself as the head of the house.

Jack Russell Terriers will test these boundaries with new people and new dogs. Make sure that you are prepared for the strong personality and assertiveness your Jack Russell may present when you are starting to socialize him. I find that it is important to start this socialization process as early as possible to make sure you have a well-rounded pup which you can be confident going into public places with.

Often, when we think of socialization, we think of socializing with other dogs and humans. This is true, but there is also what I like to call "the socialization to life" that many people don't consider. Have you ever seen a video of how blind dog training centers introduce puppies to weird things very early on in life? An umbrella opening, the dropping of a metal saucer, or even a singing stuffed animal that dances. If you haven't, I strongly recommend looking it up; not only is it cute, but it can be educational too.

These training centers do this in order to assess the reaction from the puppy and see if he maintains his calm when introduced to these strange sounds, movements, and textures. This kind of life socialization allows you to desensitize your puppy to things that might be scary. This allows him to address and approach this scary event in a safe environment, and it allows you to comfort him so that the next time he isn't as affected. This is called desensitization.

Photo Courtesy of Lietha Vermaas

Desensitization is important for a Jack Russell because he can react aggressively when he is scared and may bite or nip a person or dog because he has high emotions and is in defense mode. To start with this desensitization process, I usually like to begin with small life occurrences. Take, for example, the dropping of a metal pan; this can happen anytime while you are in the kitchen and may scare an unsocialized dog. Instead of just randomly dropping a pan on the tile floor and making a loud noise, start with dropping it on a blanket or a towel to muffle the sound a bit. This will start the initial desensitization with the concept of something big falling to the earth unexpectedly.

If my dog gets worried or nervous, maybe with his ears down and tail tucked, I will talk to him in a gentle, calm voice and say, "Oh, it's okay, buddy! You're a good boy (or girl)." I give him a cookie and some love. Once he bounces back from this initial surprise, I encourage the dog to explore and assess the fallen object. Usually, I do this by going over to the fallen pan and calling the dog to me. He may skirt the pan, but I will just sit down next to it, give him a treat, or maybe place a treat on the floor next to the pan or even on it. I allow the dog time to sniff the pan and relax around it. Usually, this can be seen with a rise in his tail, confidence in being close to the pan, and even ignoring it like it's just another part of the floor.

Once I am confident that the dog is confident, I will take the pan away and continue with my day. We don't want to overstimulate or overstress

Photo Courtesy of Julie Russon

the dog by working this desensitization repeatedly in a short period of time. Instead, I might repeat it in another thirty minutes to an hour and only do it three or four times in one day. Once he becomes indifferent to the dropping of the pan on the blanket or towel, we are done for the day. Even if the dog is indifferent, I will still tell him he is good and give him a treat, but my voice is neutral and as indifferent to the event as his behavior.

The next day, or a couple of days later, depending on how long it takes him to get comfortable, I will start dropping the pan again on the blanket or towel, and if the dog is indifferent, I will take that blanket or towel away and drop it on the floor to make the noise louder. If he gets stressed again, continue what you did after dropping it on the towel or blanket for the first time and focus on building your way up to full desensitization. If your dog is unaffected, he still gets a verbal reward and a treat. He is aware that the event happened, and if he didn't react, this is behavior that should be rewarded.

This approach can be used for all sorts of life socialization. Be creative! A stuffed animated toy is another great opportunity because it moves, sings, and is, in general, just a weird thing that can cause your Jack Russell to have all sorts of emotions. Desensitizing your dog to something like that will be a great foundation to desensitizing him to children, who are also small, make weird movements (according to your dog's perspective), and also make random unusual noises.

Do these desensitization experiences in different environments. What happens when you are together in the backyard and you put rocks in a plastic bucket? Or you start raking gravel or using power tools that are loud? These are all learning opportunities that will not only desensitize your dog but also build your relationship and trust as you move through life together.

Note, when you are doing this socialization to life, do not do it while your dog is in his crate, and make sure his crate is open and available for him just in case he gets scared! Remember, his crate is his safe space; you never want to compromise that.

Introducing your Jack Russell to new people

> *Start early. Whatever you want your Terrier to be comfortable with, be it other dogs, livestock, or small children, expose him to it immediately and often. Use caution when introducing Jack Russell adults, as they are prey-driven and may mistake other smaller breeds as quarry! For this reason, I don't usually recommend introducing an adult Terrier to livestock such as chickens.*
>
> ELLIE THOMPSON
> *Shavano Creek JRT*

In my experience, introducing Marty McFly to new people was the easiest part of his socialization. I found that Marty was very human-focused and truly acted as if he was a little human himself. When we dined outside at a restaurant, he would go to the end of his leash and wag his little nubbin at all the people walking by, especially the ladies, and we would get at least four or five people stopping to give him some love. Sometimes people would even sit on the ground and let Marty crawl into their lap! Now, I am lucky because McFly grew up surrounded by a lot of dog-savvy people who doted on him, which created this really strong positive relationship with people, but not all Jack Russell Terriers have that same upbringing.

*Photo Courtesy
of Brenda Foraie*

When your Jack Russell is young, I recommend taking him out for social-ization as much as possible. Invite people over to your house, go over to other people's houses, and give your puppy as much human exposure as possible. If your puppy or adult dog is shy, make sure you give your friends and new acquaintances high-reward treats to encourage a positive associa-tion. Also, try to be diverse in the people you socialize your dog with. Make sure it is not gender-specific. Introduce him to people in a wheelchair or using a cane, people wearing hats, sunglasses, or who have facial hair. The more diverse the people, the better.

It is also important to set boundaries with these people. If you don't, your Jack Russell will. If someone is being too rough or thinks that he is playing with your dog when in reality, he is just irritating him, let him know he needs to stop. Humans and dogs both have a specific amount of social battery. They have enough charge to handle social engagements to a certain degree before they get burned out and exhausted. Part of these socialization explorations allows you to learn where your dog's social battery lies.

Introducing your Jack Russell to new animals

> **"**
>
> *It is critical that the other dog(s) is of a similar energy level and is completely comfortable meeting new dogs. Not every dog wants a new friend! The dogs should be off-leash, and the humans should keep moving to encourage the dogs to move around and play/run. Leave toys and balls out of the mix at the start. If the other dog is already a pet in the home, I recommend that the meeting happen outside, and for extra safety, the little puppy can be in an exercise pen while the older dog sniffs him. Wagging tails are a good sign. If the older dog corrects the puppy for too much exuberance, don't scold the older dog or rescue the little puppy. Puppies have to learn their lessons from the older dogs.*
>
> PATTI STORMS
> *Rabble Rouser Jack Russell Terriers*
>
> **"**

Jack Russell Terriers love their owners very much and tend to want to be those owners' sole furry friends. If you have other animals in the home, your

Jack Russell may start to guard you from them. On walks, your Jack Russell may become leash aggressive and protective of you. These are behaviors that are not acceptable and can be curbed with socialization with other animals early on. As a caveat, just because you socialize your puppy early on doesn't mean you don't need to continue to socialize him. This is a lifelong process that requires a lot of work and very strict expectations.

Marty McFly was well socialized at a young age, but when he started getting older,

HELPFUL TIP
Can Jack Russell Terriers Be Service Dogs?

Jack Russell Terriers may not be the first dogs that come to mind when you think of service dogs. Jack Russell Terriers' dispositions aren't always ideal for service work, with their independent nature and high energy level. However, early socialization can make a massive difference if you're considering training your dog to perform a service or work as a therapy dog. Early exposure to different experiences and people is an investment in your dog's future and is crucial for raising a well-adjusted dog.

I noticed a change in his behavior, and now I am dealing with his "resource guarding" of me. Usually, what this looks like is he and I will be on the couch, watching a movie, and another dog will come up. McFly will start to growl, go into a threatening body position, and even show his teeth and snap at the other dog. This is not acceptable. As soon as he starts this behavior, he is corrected, kicked off the couch, and the other dog is invited up. McFly does not get to return to the couch until he has settled down on the floor, and I allow him to come back up.

This could have been prevented if I had kept up with his training. Though none of these instances has caused a serious event as of yet, the retraining of this behavior has been challenging, and we are working hard to remedy it. Instead of getting into my situation, let's discuss the ways you can prevent this behavior from developing in your own Jack Russell pup.

Starting this socialization process is best with dogs that you already know. Dogs that are friendly and relatively mellow are ideal. Start by meeting in a neutral place, perhaps a field or a park, and allow the two dogs to meet on leash. Watch your dog's behavior to see if he is scared, interested, or aggressively interested, and adjust your approach as needed. If things are too exciting, sit down with your dog and get him to settle into the new environment with treats. Let him take the initiative to introduce himself to the other dog. Once he has introduced himself and seems content, try socializing the two in a secure place like a backyard.

Again, start with leashes on, then let the dogs off-leash to explore and play together. Some Jack Russell Terriers will be indifferent to other dogs, but it is still important that the dogs are taught proper manners. If your Jack Russell is overexcited and bouncing all over other dogs, the other dogs may teach him as well. Allow this to happen as long as it isn't outright aggressive behavior. What I mean is, if your Jack Russell jumps all over another dog and that dog bares his teeth and gives a low grumble, he is teaching your Jack Russell to listen to dog behavioral cues. This is good. Dogs have a certain hierarchy that you cannot replicate, but your dog should be accustomed to it.

Continue these playdates with as many varieties of dogs as you can and also with other animals. McFly grew up with a kitten who was his best friend. They played together and cuddled in the same cat bed together. Unfortunately, she has since passed, but because of her, McFly learned how to behave around cats. He is respectful of them and will never doubt a cat's power if it warns him to stay away. He has also been introduced to sheep and horses and is the worst ratter in the Jack Russell world because he thinks rats are his friends. The more your dog is exposed to other creatures, the more balanced and predictable his behavior will be around new animals.

As a caveat, I personally do not recommend starting to socialize your dog at a dog park. I have had very bad experiences with other dogs at the dog park picking on McFly because of his size or straight out attacking him because he is a small dog. If you do go, I recommend going with caution and only during the unpopular times.

Puppy playdates: What to keep in mind

Though it is important to start socializing your pup at a young age, it is important to make sure that your puppy and any puppies or dogs he meets are fully vaccinated. There are harmful viruses that can be transmitted if puppies are not vaccinated.

Always try to choose a neutral environment until both parties are comfortable with one another. Make sure to encourage the pups to take timeouts for water breaks and especially if things get a little heated. This helps teach the puppies to develop a switch to "turn it off" when things are so excited. It is also ideal to let the dogs set the pace. If your Jack Russell does not want to play, don't force him to. In the end, these playdates are meant to be fun, a learning lesson, and a good medium for socialization.

Your Jack Russell and children

When introducing your Jack Russell to children, this should be a very passive interaction. It is best to educate the child or children about what your expectations are. Ideally, if the child can stay calm, allow the dog to come to him and have the child pet your Jack Russell on his side with soft, short strokes. I find the majority of Jack Russell Terriers do very well with this approach because it gives them control of the situation. Even if you do not have children, socializing your pup with them is important. Children can be loud and unpredictable, which can cause a Jack Russell anxiety, stress, and in some cases, to act aggressively out of fear. The more your dog is introduced to this unpredictability, the better.

CHAPTER EIGHT
Your Home's Hierarchy and Pack Mentality

Solidifying who is in charge

As we know, Jack Russell Terriers have a very strong personality, and if your dog is not trained to realize his place in the pecking order, he will find a way to come out on top. This is something that all dog owners should prevent from occurring because it takes the control out of your hands and puts it into your dogs' paws. There are many little things that will articulate this power dynamic, but at the end of the day, what we are looking to accomplish is to have your dog look to you for guidance.

For example, after you put the leash on your dog, does he bolt to the door, jump all over it, and dart out when you finally open it? If so, your dog is the one in charge. If your dog waits for you to open the door and looks to you for the okay to proceed, then you are in charge. This is just one very small example of how you can ensure that you are the one in charge. These learned behaviors return to our base philosophy of managing expectations and maintaining routines.

Here are some suggestions on expectations you can adapt to you and your dog's normal routine, which will solidify your position as leader.

- When it is time for your dog to eat, he should sit and wait for you to place the bowl down and release him to go eat.

- Your dog should not be allowed on the furniture until invited up. I am horribly bad with this one because I love snuggling with McFly on the couch, but it can become detrimental if he jumps up without realizing I have a bowl of popcorn in my lap.

- Ignore your dog when you come home. This is hard because he will be so excited to see you. Fly would jump all over me when I came home, get so excited he would sometimes nip, and made entering my house challenging. Now, he goes and grabs a toy, then dances around me until I get settled and invite him over for some love and conversation about the day.

- Practice stays and releases like your life depends on it. Not only does it allow for you to have control, but it can also save your dog's life if, for some reason, you become separated across a road or a river. It also is great to practice when crossing roads.

Now, these suggestions have nothing to do with the biological evolution of pack mentality but are good measures and practices of control. This distinction is important because these suggestions are not to prevent some rooted genetic behavior but are guidelines for safety and allow you to create the understanding in your dog that you have the final say in what is and is not appropriate behavior.

Photo Courtesy of Shaun and Lavina Hemming

The pack mentality

There has been a lot of research on pack mentality, and a lot of individuals have tried to connect training tips to the concepts of pack mentality in wolves to domesticated dogs. In actuality, we have bred dogs for specific traits to make them the ideal companion animals we see today. Historically, there have been training methods that use the concept of "pack mentality" to subdue or aggressively train dogs to let them learn their place in the family pack. This is just plain ignorance and bad training. If you look into trainers that use this method, I strongly recommend finding someone else.

Research has shown that wolves actually use more passive approaches to their family hierarchy. The leaders are actually the ones that make sure pups are fed first when food is minimal, and they have more of a guiding and teaching role within the pack. That is your role: you are the guide and teacher into what behavior is appropriate within your "pack."

Deciphering bad behavior or a teachable moment

To understand what bad behavior is, we have to get to the marrow of the phrase's meaning. To do something bad means that something was done that you don't like. Behavior is a repetitive habit. So bad behavior is the repetition of a behavior that you do not like. This is an important distinction because a dog may do something we consider bad, but he simply does not know that we consider it bad. For example, when McFly was young, he did not know that jumping on me right when I got home was something I hated, until one day, I got very upset about it. There were unintentionally spilled groceries on the floor, high stress, a mixture of emotions, but he didn't know because I did not teach him that I didn't like him to jump all over me. Now, if he had kept on doing this behavior to spite me, which dogs rarely do, though Jack Russells can

HISTORICAL FACT
Origins

Jack Russell Terriers can be traced back to a dog named Trump. Purchased by Reverend John Russell in 1815 from the milkman, this dog became the foundation for a line of working Terriers used for fox hunting. The reverend continued to crossbreed with other white Terriers to produce a dog who would be able to bark and nip at a fox, forcing it to bolt but not killing it.

sometimes be the exception to the rule, I would call this a bad behavior.

There is always a teaching moment, but these moments are not just for your dog. They are also for you. Your dog is not going to learn what you desire unless you are clear about your expectations. If you sometimes let him jump up on you with no correction and then at other times get overly upset by him jumping on you, this is hard for him to learn because he is getting mixed messages. Clear and consistent expectations are key to reducing or eliminating unwanted behavior.

Photo Courtesy of Brenda Foraie

Positive reinforcement is the best way to educate a dog. If you are always using punishment, you may still eliminate a behavior, but it may be replaced by another bad behavior or a breakdown in the relationship with your dog. We want to end these behaviors but also enhance the bond we have with our dogs. If you feel overwhelmed, as I sure have, step outside, walk away from your dog, and come back when you are ready. It is better to miss a moment to teach than to do something that could be detrimental to your relationship.

Working through tough relationships between pets

Sometimes there can be tensions between pets in the home, and this can be an extreme challenge to deal with. Usually, we try to mitigate these challenges in the beginning by introducing new additions to the home through meet and greets in a neutral environment. However, it is impossible to fully assess how two pets will get along in the home environment for the entirety of their lives. Relationships change over time, and though relationships usually get better between pets, they sometimes can also develop more tension and stress.

When you first start to notice a negative change in your pets' relationships, it is good to try to get a whole picture of the situation. Did your dog snap at the cat because he was chewing on a bone when the cat walked by? If so, this could be resource guarding, which could mean some additional training and reeducation on expectations may be needed. Did your Jack Russell all of a sudden attack your other dog, completely out of the blue? Maybe there is an underlying health condition that has arisen that needs to be addressed. Does your Jack Russell now growl at anything else that tries to get close to you when he is snuggling you on the couch? (I am looking at you, Marty McFly). Maybe you have let this behavior develop incrementally over time, and you now need to pay more attention to prevent it from happening.

No matter what occurs, it is important to see what led up to the event, how your dog reacted, and then what happened directly after. Sometimes things happen that you had no idea about because your dog was never placed in that situation before. These can be challenging events, but there is always something to be learned from as well. I had a foster once who was great with my cat because my cat never ran from dogs. She knew to stand her ground, and all of our fosters respected her for that.

However, this one particular foster got adopted, and there was a cat in the home who did run away from dogs. Unfortunately, when the cat ran, the dog followed, and this led to an injury. Nobody was particularly

Photo Courtesy
of Nina Chang and Brooke Lloyd

at fault in this scenario, but it did teach both the dog's new owners and me that proper introductions should be made, and when unsupervised, household pets should be separated, especially during the introductory weeks.

Photo Courtesy of Kimberly Kan

Jack Russell Terriers can be a bit high-strung, and I always recommend that they are given their own personal space, especially when they are home alone with other pets. You never know what may occur during the day that could trigger any of your pets, and this may lead to injury or the further development of tensions. Part of this could be that your pets are not getting enough exercise and are trying to burn off energy on each other instead.

Try adding additional walks or intense play times for a couple of weeks to see if that helps tire your pets out. Sometimes jealousy, especially in Jack Russell Terriers, can be a cause. To address this, try to have individual time with each of your pets. This can be in the form of individual training or play sessions for ten minutes a day or taking them on individual walks. If tough relationships between pets continue to occur, after you have tried further training, additional exercise, and one-on-one sessions with each pet, I strongly recommend going to a vet to discuss metabolic issues or behavioral modification recommendations.

CHAPTER NINE

The Physical and Mental Exercise Needed for Your Jack Russell

Physical exercise requirements and tips

> "
>
> *Jack Russell Terriers need exercise, and they have a lot of energy. Many people like a Terrier as a jogging buddy, hiking companion, or like to compete in agility and field trials. Families can include them in activities like errands and chores and daily walks. If that's not possible, most Terriers will play ball endlessly! Mental exercises like scattering kibble instead of feeding in a bowl will cause your JRT to use his nose to 'hunt' for his food. This is a favorite at our kennel! Many canine feeding games are available online as well. You will find that Terriers like a regular schedule and will likely learn yours. Your JRT will look forward to his daily routine and the love you give him and will happily show up for his walk or feeding time like clockwork!*
>
> ELLIE THOMPSON
> *Shavano Creek JRT*
>
> "

Jack Russell Terriers are a breed that needs a lot of exercise because they were bred in order to chase prey during a hunt for long periods of time and in all types of terrain. Without having an outlet for their energy needs,

Photo Courtesy of Billie Jo Sage

Jack Russell Terriers will find a way to expel this pent-up energy, which may be destructive in nature. They are a breed that needs to be both physically and mentally exercised.

The Jack Russell breed is very intelligent. In fact, I believe they are too smart for their own good, and their attitude also makes them real characters. Jack Russell Terriers love to figure out puzzles and need to have their minds stimulated as much as their tiny bodies.

I really feel blessed with Marty McFly. He has a well-balanced drive, as well as the ability to turn his energy level and excitement on and off based on what our activities are for the day. That being said, I am a relatively active person and bring him along for all the adventures I can. This may make his energy level seem more manageable for me. Someone who lives in an apartment and is working all the time may find that getting their Jack Russell to turn off his or her energy and excitement is a lot more challenging.

McFly and I currently live a ten-minute walk from the boardwalk and the beach. We walk and play on the beach almost every morning, go on walks around our neighborhood every evening, and adventure on our days off. I also include McFly on a variety of adventures. He has a basket he sits in when we go biking. We go paddleboarding together. He is my first mate while flat-water kayaking, and the two of us are constantly looking for new hiking trails and camping sites. Even when we go into the city, McFly rides in my backpack on the train and navigates the streets alongside me.

It was my goal to find a dog that matched my lifestyle when I started looking into the Jack Russell breed. I already did a lot of these activities but wanted to share them with someone. I had worked with larger breeds like Border Collies before, but I wanted a more portable dog, which led me to this breed.

Your lifestyle is going to be a big factor in fulfilling your Jack Russell's exercise requirements. If you work long hours and tend to be a homebody, a Jack Russell may not be the dog for you, but I say this only as a generality. You may find that an older Jack Russell rescue might be more suiting and less energetic. In the end, it is

HELPFUL TIP
Energy Level

Jack Russell Terriers are high-energy dogs who can seem to have boundless energy and need several walks or play sessions per day. As working dogs, Jack Russells thrive when given a job, so diligent training is a must with this breed. They make excellent running or jogging companions and can be great candidates for agility training.

Photo Courtesy
of Aleksandar Mishkov

always better to find a dog that matches your lifestyle than trying to change your lifestyle to match your dog's.

Trying to find ways to expend my dog's energy is one of my favorite things to do. There are tons of ways to play with your dog that burn off energy and also challenge them mentally. Of course, there are traditional ways of exercising dogs, such as going to a park to play fetch and taking them for a walk or a run or a hike. These are great ideas that you can use to burn off excess energy. However, there are also other fun things you can do that tap into your Jack Russell's natural instincts.

Earlier, I mentioned playing hide-and-seek with McFly. I often do this at home, but I have even done this at the dog park or on a hike. When we are at home and he is sleeping, I will get up and sneak off to hide behind a door, in a closet, or behind the shower curtain, and then I will call to him. He will bolt up and start searching the house for me. I always end up giving myself away because he is so cute when he is on "the hunt," and I can't help but giggle.

> **"**
>
> *Once a Jack is physically mature, hiking and running with his owner can be very enjoyable. If the Jack has a large fenced yard, he can keep himself busy for hours digging holes, chasing squirrels, and exploring on his own. In the house, Jacks are typically quiet (unless the UPS man comes or a squirrel is heard) and enjoy just being near you. An adult dog usually needs about one hour of some type of outdoor activity per day. JRTs can excel in sports like agility, barn hunt, canicross, and dock diving, for example. One of the best mental games for them is scent work or nose work.*
>
> GINA E. SNOW
> *Swanback Jacks*
>
> **"**

Play a game of "find it." This is a simple game where you can take your dog's favorite toy and hide it while you tell your pup to wait in one room or in his crate. To really activate McFly's hunting instinct, I use small bits of fox pelts, which still hold the fox scent. I will hide these behind a pillow on the couch, in the folds of a blanket, or in a basket. Then I will return to McFly and release him, tell him to "find it," and let him search the house for the fox pelt. Once he finds it, I let him play and tear at it for a couple of minutes. I then hide it again and repeat the process a couple more times but stop before he gets bored.

Take your Jack Russell on a water-based adventure. Swimming burns a ton of energy, both for humans and their canine counterparts. A sit-on-top kayak or a paddleboard gives you more freedom and less wetness and allows your Jack Russell to jump off for a swim and come back on when he needs a break. When doing water sports, I always make sure McFly has his personal flotation device (PFD) on. A PFD is important because it gives your dog extra support while swimming, and PFDs usually have a handle on them in case you need to grab the dog quickly.

Photo Courtesy of Rebecca & Gabe Morales

In order to hone into the Jack Russell prey drive, I use an interactive chase and drag toy that looks like a pole with a string at one end. The other end of the string usually has a toy or an animal pelt your dog can chase after.

I find that scheduling puppy play dates also helps dramatically with burning off energy. It also allows your pup to interact with other dogs and refines his socialization skills with his peers. I make sure to schedule these play dates with other dogs McFly and I know and are comfortable with because he can be dramatic with dogs he doesn't have a relationship with. These playdates are often us going to a friend's house and drinking wine on the patio while the dogs run around the backyard chasing after toys we toss. This is what I like to call a win-win exercise plan!

Mental exercise and its importance

> *There are a lot of wonderful outlets for mentally engaging your Jack Russell. There are many toys and puzzles on the market just for this purpose. Short training exercises are also a great way to stimulate your dog and keep him engaged. Playing games with a ball, taking him to agility or obstacle courses, participating in nose work exercises, and many other activities that combine physical activity that will engage your dog's mind are available in most areas. If these are not available, you can make up your own versions at home. Country dogs love to ride with you, check on the cows, go to the barn. Really, anything that interests the dog and allows him to be with you can be turned into an activity. The worst thing is to turn a JRT out into the yard alone without anything to do. This is when he will create his own activities, and those are not usually choices that are pleasing to humans.*
>
> WENDY PALMER
> *Thistle Ridge Terriers*

Multiple times I have heard people say that their dogs never seem to be satisfied no matter how much they exercise them. When I inquire into what type of dog people have, almost ten out of ten times, the dog is some sort of hunting or working breed. These intelligent breeds with high energy need more than just physical exercise; they need mental exercise. Mental exercise means that your dog has to use his mind in order to complete a task.

There are many ways to stimulate and work your Jack Russell's mind, some of which I have discussed above, but there is also a lot of room for creativity. I am lucky to have a local Jack Russell Terrier Club where McFly participates in many activities. Look into potential clubs in your area, and see if your Jack Russell loves one of the events that they offer. There are multiple types of competitions that are specifically created for the Jack Russell breed, such as Super Earth and Jack Russell racing events.

Another idea to keep your dog mentally stimulated is to have him work for one meal a day using a snuffle mat or a puzzle board, which are interactive feeding games for your dog.

Bring your dog to the jungle gym at the park and have him climb up the stairs and slide down the slides. This gets him comfortable with different environments, physically challenges him, and makes him use his brain to navigate different terrain. Imagine doggie parkour! Note—this is best done at times when children are not around.

Photo Courtesy of Rebecca Allan

Teach your dog the different names of his toys. Once your dog knows each toy's name, put all the toys in a basket and ask him to get a specific toy. Or instead of the basket, you can spread the toys out around the house and ask him to get a specific toy. The dog will then have to search the house for the toy and bring it to you.

Blow bubbles in the backyard for your dog to chase. If you have kids, this can be an activity that can entertain both your dogs and your kids!

Train your dog to do "chores" around the house. This can be him picking up things from the floor and bringing them to you. You can also teach your dog to close and open cabinet doors and even to put his toys away.

> **"**
>
> *Mental exercise tires out a Jack far more than physical. Practicing obedience homework, teaching the dog tricks, or a walk in the woods over lots of uneven terrain will make the Jack Russell think as well as move. Ball or Frisbee playing is great, but Jacks can get a bit compulsive about it and play until they literally drop. Playing ball can be used as a reward rather than as the sole way of exercising the dog. Variety is key!*
>
> PATTI STORMS
> *Rabble Rouser Jack Russell Terriers*
>
> **"**

CHAPTER TEN

The Building Blocks of Training

> **"**
>
> *Jack Russell Terriers are very intelligent. Since they were originally bred to 'work' a quarry underground and think on their own, you will find that they do the same in your home! Your dog will spend a lot of time watching and thinking and figuring things out. He will also try to anticipate your every move. He will test your boundaries to see if that rule really was meant for him...or if you simply made a mistake making that rule. Jack Russell Terriers are extremely loyal and loving but will constantly test the boundaries to see what more they can do!*
>
> ELLIE THOMPSON
> *Shavano Creek JRT*
>
> **"**

Standing by your expectations

We have talked about standing by your expectations and standards time and time again, but this is especially true when it comes to training. When you ask for a specific behavior, the dog should obey. I never ask more than three times before I take a different approach. These expectations must also be maintained throughout the years with your dog. When your standards start to slide, so will your dog's response.

Positive reinforcement and operant conditioning

> *Jacks learn quickly and do not forget. So, tricks and training can be easily picked up. They often do not need or enjoy lots of training drills. Keep things moving with action, and keep an upbeat attitude, and they should learn easily. If they are not learning easily, it's likely to become unfun for them.*
>
> GINA E. SNOW
> *Swanback Jacks*

Positive reinforcement means marking good behavior with a positive response. When your dog sits, and you say, "good sit," and give him a treat, this is positive reinforcement. On the opposite side, negative reinforcement is when the only consequence is that something is taken away. For example, you take away the shoe your puppy was chewing on and don't give him a different and appropriate toy to chew on.

Positive and negative reinforcement has been thoroughly researched, and all the results lead to the understanding that positive reinforcement is

always more effective than negative. However, positive reinforcement is not as easy as just praising your dog when he does something good. There are some key tricks to make positive reinforcement the most effective type of training for you and your dog.

Make sure your timing is on point. Instantly, after your dog performs the behavior requested, you must mark this with a positive cue like "yes" or "good" and perhaps even follow it with a treat. The faster this reward is provided after the requested behavior is performed, the stronger the association between the behavior and the reward becomes.

Be short and concise with your commands. One-word commands are best. If you use a whole sentence to ask for a behavior, your dog is going to be confused.

Use positive reinforcement for behaviors you have specifically requested. When training your dog, he may offer a behavior that he is confident with, such as sitting when you are asking for him to lie down. Other forms of

Photo Courtesy
of Aleksandar Mishkov

unintentional positive reinforcement could also be letting your dog out when he barks at a noise outside. The behavior you don't want is barking, and you are reinforcing this by letting him outside.

Operant conditioning is similar to positive reinforcement but is essentially the association made between a behavior and a consequence. The consequence for operant conditioning can be positive or negative, unlike positive reinforcement, which only recognizes desirable behaviors. Operant conditioning is the way puppies and children discover life and what is okay and not okay to do. For example, if a puppy runs up to a cat and that cat smacks him with his claws and scares the puppy, he is going to learn that cat equals claws, which then equals pain, and he will learn not to run up to the cat again. If you ask your dog, "want to go for a walk?" and then you get him all excited about going for a walk, he is going to associate that term with being allowed to get excited and then being rewarded for this excitement by going for a walk.

Clicker training is a good example of how to use operant conditioning for positive reinforcement training in your dog. The clicker itself marks a positive behavior with a sound and lets the dog know that he is going to receive a treat. First, the dog must learn to associate the sound of the click with treats, and then the clicker can be introduced into training. The dog does the behavior requested, hears the click, and a reward follows. This is really helpful when you begin doing training at a distance.

Secondary reinforcements

Secondary reinforcements can appear in many different ways. For Marty McFly and me, these usually take the form of major playtime or a tug-of-war battle. For example, Marty and I may be doing agility, and I ask him to go over a jump. His initial reward is the toss of his favorite tug toy. He runs to fetch it and then returns to me and gets pets while he holds his toy. Then we tug for a minute or so. Jack Russell Terriers love this form of reinforcement, or at least mine does, because it is all about him and praising him.

Note that when Marty returns with his toy, I do not take it away from him right away. This is because him holding that toy is a reward, and I want to extend that reward time to emphasize his good behavior. He hates it when I take the toy away, so why would I do that if I am trying to reward him? Now, some Jack Russell Terriers may love playing fetch, so it would be appropriate to grab a toy and toss it again if a dog prefers that treat. To each his own.

Why negative reinforcement can be harmful to training

The name gives it away, but negative reinforcement is just that—negative. If it is used often as a training tool, it will break down the relationship you have with your dog and will make training harder. Jack Russell Terriers are especially a breed in which negative reinforcement can be detrimental and may backfire on you.

Note that negative reinforcement is often confused with punishment. Punishment is a verbal or physical action a dog receives when he does something an owner doesn't like. This could be pushing a dog's nose in pee when he urinates in the house, for example. This is never appropriate or helpful when training your dog. Conversely, negative reinforcement can also be a removal of a negative outcome that serves as a reward for a behavior, such as a dog sniffing a crab and getting a pinch on the nose. The pinch is a negative outcome, so in order to remove that negative outcome a dog will learn not to go sniffing crabs. This type of negative reinforcement uses fear and even pain to create a behavior. In humans, this is easy to distinguish because it could be as simple as learning to put on sunscreen after spending a day at the beach without it and having to deal with the burn after.

The negative reinforcement was a horrible sunburn, and the behavioral change was to put sunscreen on.

For some dogs, an example of this could be rattlesnake training. An owner will place the scent of a rattlesnake down or have a defanged snake in a cage. When the dog goes to sniff the snake, he will receive a shock on a shock collar or hear a loud rattle from a can filled with pennies. The goal is to create a traumatic negative association between the smell and the snake to reduce rattlesnake bites. It works, but it can also traumatize a dog to the point that he can't go on hikes or may dread that type of environment.

Puppy classes

Puppy classes are wonderful to attend no matter what level of training ability you have. These classes provide an environment in which you can challenge your puppy to learn under very distracting circumstances. They allow you to learn how to teach under these circumstances and are a good experience for everyone involved. I also find puppy classes help with things my puppy or I are struggling with because there is a third person who can see what is going on and who can suggest a simple change that may make a huge difference. This also allows you to teach your dog in a safe environment with someone who is experienced with dogs and training. Lastly, such classes are a great social event for both you and your dog, and you may be able to create relationships outside of the class.

When looking into puppy classes, there are some things you may want to consider. Read the biography of the instructor or trainer. Look to see what

FUN FACT
HMV Logo Dog

His Master's Voice or HMV is a large United Kingdom–based record label that's been in operation since 1921. The widely recognizable logo for this company features a dog looking into the speaker of a gramophone. The dog in this logo is based on a real-life Jack Russell Terrier mix named Nipper. Nipper was owned by a painter named Francis Barraud, who painted his dog listening to a gramophone in 1899 and titled the painting *His Master's Voice*. The painting was purchased by the Gramophone Company, which opened the first HMV branded store, and it was adapted into their logo.

his experience is and/or what kinds of dogs he has. See if he teaches any other types of classes or participates in dog activities, such as competing in dog sports or volunteering with a rescue organization.

I always like to look into what kind of environment I will be attending classes in. A lot of big-name pet stores have classes in stores, and though this isn't necessarily a bad thing, I prefer to have something a little less distracting. I have attended puppy classes in converted garages, in parks, and in someone else's home and found that all these locations have positives and negatives. Find whatever you think is going to be best for you and your puppy.

Photo Courtesy of Shelby Queen

Some puppy classes are open to anyone and don't have any limitations except an age requirement. Other classes may be for small breeds only or for puppies between a specific age range. These can be helpful if you are finding training has been a bit more difficult than anticipated, or if you feel like your dog may be more comfortable with a smaller range of class-mate variation. If you can find a trainer who is acquainted with Jack Russell Terriers or a class that is geared toward smaller breeds or Terrier breeds, I recommend taking a look because those classes may provide more specific training based on your needs.

How to be the best owner, trainer, and handler for your pup

You have already started on the journey to being the best owner, trainer, and handler for your pup because you are actively seeking advice and guidance. In the end, loving your Jack Russell for all that he is, the good, the bad, and the furry, will make you a good dog parent. Dogs need food, water, a home, and someone to love them. Jack Russell Terriers can be a challenging breed—trust me, I know—and sometimes I tell McFly that I love him, but I don't really like him right now. This is okay, and honestly, sometimes you need to walk away, especially when your dog is being obnoxious. That is also being a good dog owner because you're setting limits and barriers.

CHAPTER ELEVEN

Seven Basic Commands Your Jack Russell Should Know

Why training is so important

> *Jack Russells are very smart. My friend says Jacks are too smart for most people. They are creative and need to learn boundaries. As a breeder, I start my puppies with some basic clicker training and encourage new owners to continue with formal obedience training classes. An untrained Terrier will likely develop unwanted behaviors and get into mischief.*
>
> BETTYANN SENF
> *Candeejack Terriers*

Training allows you to take your dog to more places and makes him an active member of your family. If your dog isn't trained and you have people over and he's jumping all over them, or you feel like you have to lock him in a room, he won't be able to be an active member of your home. Marty McFly is an important member of my family. He is a part of my day-to-day routine, but he is also a part of my vacations and holidays. Training was the pathway to get him to that point.

Choosing the best rewards for your dog

Your dog is going to let you know what he likes and what he doesn't. If you are getting a puppy, you usually will have some flexibility because he'll initially be a blank slate. If you adopt an older dog, he may have preferences, such as not liking dog toys. Trust me—he will let you know.

For training purposes, I always try to use high-reward treats that McFly only gets during training. These can be something as simple as cheese cubes or as fancy as freeze-dried liver or chicken hearts. Whatever you choose, make sure your dog only gets it while training to make the reward that much more valuable.

Also, if you are doing a lot of training, make sure to watch your dog's weight. An older dog doesn't burn as many calories as a developing puppy, so extra treats can add a significant number of calories to his diet. If I do a heavy training day that is not filled with a ton of physical activity, I will reduce one dog meal by 10–25%. I feed McFly twice a day, and when I plan to do training one day, I will skip his breakfast and "make him earn his meal" through training. These are days where he is starving to please me, literally, and I can get some good training in. I also tend to be heavy-handed on my treats, so the calorie totals balance out the missed meal.

I use a combination of treats and toys with McFly, depending on what type of training we are doing. If I am focusing on agility, there are going to be a lot of toys involved because there is a lot of distance work in that training. It is much easier to toss a toy for him to go after than a treat. There are also toys that are secret treat bags so you can have an all-in-one toy, which some dogs absolutely love.

Basic commands

There are some basic commands that every dog should know in order to make him an active member of a household and civil when he is out in society. This helps you protect him from potential dangers, builds the relationship you have with your dog, and allows you to have the freedom to take him to a more diverse range of places and settings.

When training in the following basic commands, I try to get a couple of short sessions in every day until they are solidified. I recommend only working on one command during a session until you have a few that are pretty solid. Make sure that each session is no longer than ten minutes. This helps prevent burn-out in your dog and allows sessions to be as impactful as possible. Training can become longer later on, but when learning something new, small, bite-sized pieces are best.

Sit

This is probably the most common command and is usually the first command dogs learn. It is natural for a dog to sit, and all you really have to do is teach him to do this natural behavior upon your request. For a Jack Russell, I usually teach this command by sitting on the floor and having the dog in front of me. I will then take the treat, let the dog sniff it, and slowly bring it up and over his head while saying, "sit." You may also need to take your other hand and gently put pressure on his rear to solidify the request.

As soon as the dog sits, praise him. Say, "Good sit," reinforcing the command, and make sure he gets a treat. Try this again right after and use

Photo Courtesy of Rebecca Allan

pressure on his rear only if the dog needs it. The goal is to get rid of that support as soon as possible. Once the dog starts using this behavior, I will try to challenge him by requesting it randomly throughout the day, in different environments, and with distractions to make sure the command is solid.

Lie Down (or Down)

Usually, I just use "down" for this command, but if McFly is challenging me, he will get a strong verbal "LIE DOWN" from me, which usually gets the point across that I am serious about my command. There are two schools of thought to teaching this command. The first is having your dog start by getting his front half down first, almost in a play bow, and then placing pressure on his rear to get him to drop into a lying position.

The second school of thought is that your dog has already learned sit, so you should put him into a sit and then ask him to lie down while you bring the treat to the floor and encourage the dog to drop down on his front legs into a lying position. Neither method is right or wrong. Try one and see how your dog does with it. I personally use the sit-to-down technique because it is a little more hands-off, and I have also never seen a dog lie down going elbows first, followed by rear.

Stay/Wait

"Stay" and "wait" can have the same actional behavior but mean different lengths of time. When I tell McFly to wait, that means that there are moments of pause until his release. "Stay" means he must not leave a spot until directed otherwise, which can be several minutes or longer. When teaching stay, I usually start with our solidified "sit" command, then once McFly sits, I immediately say, "stay," and then take a step back. If he follows, I say, "Uh-oh," and repeat, "Sit. Stay," and step back. Once it clicks that he cannot get up from his sit, I say, "good stay," release him with an "okay," and give him a treat.

I build this up until I can walk to the end of the leash or the other side of the backyard. Then I do it all over with the down command.

For "wait," I usually practice during walks and playtime. On a walk, I will tell McFly to wait before we go through a door or cross a street. He learns this behavior because he is also reading my body language. I tell him, "wait," while I stop moving forward, so he also stops moving forward. During playtime, I will take his toy from him, tell him to wait, then place his toy in front

Photo Courtesy
of Shaun and Lavina Hemming

of him and say, "okay." He'll spring onto his toy, and we have a wonderful round of keep-away or tug-of-war.

For "wait," I do not have a specific positional requirement, meaning I do not require McFly to be sitting or lying down. On walks, he usually is standing when I tell him to wait, and during playtime, he usually lies down because he loves to spring up and pounce on his toy.

Come

This command is to get your dog to come back to you, and in my definition, I include no matter what. I usually teach this on leash because it allows me to have some control of the situation. Take your dog for a walk, then, at some random point, call your dog's name, followed immediately by "come" and stop your forward movement. The calling of your dog's name will have him look at you; your stopping of forward movement will make him have to come back to you, where you should have a reward ready for him. It takes a little mental preparation on your part, but dogs usually pick it up quickly.

Leave it

I often use this command in conjunction with "come." If McFly is totally excited about something, and I don't want him to interact with it, I tell him to leave it and then come so we can get away from the object. I start teaching "leave it" by sitting on the floor and having my dog sit in front of me; then, I place a treat on my knee. The dog automatically wants to go after it, but I cover it with my hand or take it away at the same time I say, "Leave it."

In the wild dog hierarchy, dogs learn to wait until they are given permission to eat by the alpha, so this is something that they tend to learn easily. Once your dog has gotten the hang of "leave it" in this context, turn it up a notch by taking him on a walk in the house with fun things on the floor like toys

HELPFUL TIP
Guinness World Record Holder

A Jack Russell Terrier from California named Twinkie holds the record for fastest time to pop 100 balloons, 39.08 seconds. Twinkie smashed the previous record of 41.67 seconds set in 2015. Twinkie's mother held this same record from 2005 to 2015.

Photo Courtesy
of Jacqueline Robson

or treats. Having the leash allows you to prevent the dog from getting the reward without permission.

Eventually, you can work your way up to going outside, off-leash, and walking around the yard with all sorts of distractions. This is a lifelong practice that can literally save your dog's life. Say you drop a toxic food item in the kitchen while cooking, and your dog runs to eat it, but you say, "Leave it," and he actually does! Not only did you save yourself from a potentially expensive vet bill, but you could actually save your dog's life.

I worked in veterinary medicine for over ten years, and I saw a lot of pets who accidentally ingested something toxic. A small dog like a Jack Russell can be poisoned more easily than other dogs. Chocolate, especially high percentage baking chocolate, tends to be the most common concern, but so are things like ibuprofen, which are small tablets that can easily fall. "Leave it" buys you time to find whatever you might have dropped that can have terrible repercussions for your dog should he ingest it.

Off

This command can mean "stop jumping on me," "get off the furniture," etc. Remember when I was talking about how McFly used to jump on me when I got home? Well, off was the command he learned to stop that behavior. When your dog jumps on you, say, "off," and turn your body away from him, then repeat-repeat-repeat, until he understands the association. As soon as his front paws are on the ground, say, "good off," and then turn back toward your dog. If he jumps up again, repeat your "off" and turn.

Teaching your dog to get off furniture is much easier. You can place him on your couch, then tell him "off." I usually throw a treat or cookie onto the floor when I say "off" for added motivation.

Give/Drop it

"Give to me" means my dog needs to put whatever is in his mouth into my hand. "Drop it" means that my dog must drop whatever is in his mouth onto the floor or ground. It is important that your dog understands one of these commands because he may get ahold of something that he should not have, and you need him to get it out of his mouth immediately. It also is great for when you just want to play an awesome game of fetch.

The best way to teach this is during play. I usually use a plush or rope toy to play tug with McFly, and then I will tell him to "give." If he doesn't, I will grab the toy on either side of his mouth and hold it there, repeating the command. This is no fun for him, and as soon as he lets go of the toy, he gets a "good give," and I return the toy to him. The association is the sooner he drops it, the sooner he gets it back.

Advanced commands

There are a lot more commands and tricks that you can teach your dog. It is good for Jack Russell Terriers to continually learn and be challenged. A lot of the more advanced tricks and commands McFly has learned were a combination of what I thought would be cool and what he already offered up. He has learned to spin to the right and the left, which I think every Jack Russell is bound to learn due to the breed's energetic level. In addition to this, McFly is very vocal when he plays with me, so I shaped this behavior into a command. Now when I ask him to whisper, he gives me a low growl. He doesn't like his paws being touched, so no matter how much I try, he refuses to learn "shake." Other tricks he has learned are to open and close a cabinet and to dance.

Continuing to educate your dog will help keep him entertained and mentally exercised throughout his life, which is an essential part of owning a Jack Russell Terrier.

CHAPTER TWELVE

Competing With Your Jack Russell

>
> *There are many activities that provide both physical and mental exercise. For example, there are various training classes, such as basic obedience, rally, agility, and nose work. There are Jack Russell trials where the dogs can do racing and play simulated hunting games. Dogs that like to swim and retrieve do very well at dock diving.*
>
> BETTYANN SENF
> *Candeejack Terriers*
>

Introduction to competing with your Jack Russell

One of the best things I ever did with Marty McFly was to take him to a Jack Russell Terrier Club event. This was an event hosted by our local Jack Russell Terrier club that had multiple sports and activities you could try with your Jack Russell, as well as being full of vendors and other Jack Russells. McFly got to participate in all sorts of Jack Russell–specific sports, and I got to talk to people who also understand the unique experience of being a Jack Russell owner. This was the best way to get introduced to competing events and the breed itself.

I highly recommend finding a local Jack Russell Terrier club to see what activities and programs it offers. Plus, this will give you firsthand access to Jack Russell experts who can share their experience and knowledge of the breed.

Photo Courtesy of Julie Russon

Competing with your dog takes you to a whole different level of dog ownership. It changes your relationship into a partnership, and you and your dog become a team in the arena. Training for competition, even training in a dog sport for fun, is going to have its challenges, but it is a great way to spend time with your dog. Before I got McFly, I had worked with dogs in multiple sports, everything from hunting to confirmation to flyball, but I had never experienced any Jack Russell–specific sports before. McFly, however, did not excel at any of these sports—and I partially blame myself for this—and he just didn't have that intense hunting drive that other Jack Russell Terriers did. During the barn hunt, when the dogs have to go look and find the rat hidden in a tube, McFly found it and literally became friends with the rat. Meanwhile, the other Jack Russell Terriers were digging and biting at the tube with all the power their little bodies could muster. To each his own.

Conformation events

Conformation events are what most people think when they hear the words "dog show." If the Westminster Dog show popped into your head as you read those words, you would be exactly right. This kind of event judges each dog for how close it is to the breed standard. The judges look at conformation and movement but also temperament.

Photo Courtesy of Jenny Verschuur

Racing

Racing is a very fun event in the Jack Russell world. This event has a straight course in which Jack Russell Terriers are placed in individual boxes at one end of the course, and at the other end of the course, there is a stack of straw bales with a hole big enough for one dog to go through. The dogs are usually muzzled for safety because intensity and emotional levels are high. There is a lure on a string that is pulled from the box through the hole in order to give the Terriers something to chase.

The dogs are released at the sound of a bell, and they all tear down the track after the lure toward the hole in the bales. The first dog in wins. These competitions can be run in a series of heats, semis, and finals. Some races may even include hurdles.

McFly did not like this event. As soon as he was released, he turned right around and panicked because he couldn't find me. I had to go back to the beginning to retrieve him because he could not care less about the lure and just wanted to get to me. Needless to say, we did not win.

Go-To-Ground

This is a very fun event that really triggers hunting instincts in Jack Russell Terriers by simulating a hunting situation. There is a tunnel system the dog enters in search of his quarry. Within the tunnel are several turns and dead ends to make it harder for the Terrier. Once he finds his quarry, he must give a signal by barking, scratching, or whining within the allotted amount of time in order to qualify.

Agility

This event has a host of obstacles set up that the handler has to direct the dog through in a specific pattern as fast as possible without any faults. This competition takes lots of training and is an excellent way for both the handler and the dog to get exercise. This is my personal favorite dog sport,

Photo Courtesy of Julie Russon

and McFly and I love to compete in it. This sport does take a lot of time and patience to be successful at, but the benefits are amazing, and the connection you develop with your dog is unlike any other dog sport out there.

Obedience

This is another sport that involves both the handler and the dog's participation. The dog and the handler are required to perform a series of exercises that are meant to test the obedience of the dog. There is a judge who critiques your dog's obedience and responsiveness to your commands. This is a great way to show and challenge your dog's skills, but I find that it is not as exciting and fun as some other sports.

FUN FACT
Muskrat Racing

Muskrat racing is a non-titled event for Jack Russell Terriers that is sometimes offered as a fun activity in conjunction with other competitions. Hunting muskrats is something that Jack Russell Terriers have taken part in for hundreds of years, but have no fear; muskrat racing poses no risk to these small rodents. An artificial muskrat lure is pulled through water where Jack Russell Terriers dive from a dock and give chase. These events are sometimes held in municipal pools or local ponds and can be great exercise and fun for your Terrier.

CHAPTER THIRTEEN
Redirecting Unwanted Behaviors

Defining unwanted behaviors

Often when we get a dog, we think about all of the tricks and commands we want him to know. However, we may forget to define what behaviors we do not want our dog to exhibit. Instead, what usually happens is our dog does something that we don't like, and then we try to address it at that moment. In that precise moment of time, we often tell a dog, "no!" and then give him no further direction.

Finding the root of the behavior

The most important part of stopping unwanted behaviors is looking for the root of the behavior and managing it through prevention practices. This eradicates opportunities for your dog to practice the behavior and make it a habit. First, label what the unwanted behavior is. Does your dog chew on your shoes? Whenever the neighbor walks by, does your dog bark? Once you define the unwanted behavior, then you need to decide what behavior you would prefer your dog to do instead.

Dogs may be expressing normal dog behaviors when they are doing something you don't like. Perhaps your dog is barking at someone walking in front of the house. The barking may be annoying, but your dog is doing it for a reason, alerting his pack to a stranger. Sometimes these unwanted behaviors are a product of anxiety, and a dog is trying to alleviate nervousness with behaviors such as digging at the door. Sometimes dogs do things that we consider bad behavior but that they find really fun. For example, Marty McFly loves jumping up on me, especially when I return home from work, and I hate it because he scratches me with his toenails. He doesn't mean to hurt or annoy me; he is just very excited. Another root of these

*Photo Courtesy
of Jillian & Robert Garnett*

behaviors may be from frustration or fear, such as barking for no known reason, tearing up the carpet, or peeing in the house.

Consider what outcome the dog is trying to get by demonstrating this unwanted behavior. Perhaps he is trying to get your attention, and that is why he is jumping up on you. Maybe he is bored when you are gone, so he gets into the garbage for entertainment. This outcome is what ends up reinforcing that unwanted behavior, and it is important to distinguish these reinforcements and remove them and then provide the dog with an alternate outlet.

Fixing the bad habit

Defining what you would like your dog to do instead of the unwanted behavior and then teaching him this alternate outlet for his energy will make it easier for everyone. For example, instead of jumping up on me, I have Marty McFly grab a toy and keep all four paws on the floor until I invite him up. Or, instead of chewing my shoes, I want him to chew on his toys. So on and so forth. By finding and defining what we would like our dogs to do instead of the specific undesirable behavior, we are defining a goal to work toward. This allows us to create a training plan.

Part of changing an unwanted behavior is to change the environment. If your dog chews on your shoes, you may need to find a place to put them where your dog can't get to them. If your dog barks excessively at people walking by the front of the house, you may need to incorporate a screen or curtain to block the view. You may need to reinforce crate training or add baby gates to your doorways to prevent access to certain areas of the home. This is especially common in kitchen areas to prevent dogs from getting into the garbage or counter surfing.

Add a positive interrupter to your training toolbox. A positive interrupter is a word or noise that tells your dog that he needs to stop what he is doing and engage with you. This allows you to not only get him to stop the behavior but to redirect his energy. If you do not redirect this energy, he may turn back to that undesired behavior. This positive interrupter is relatively easy to train and solidify in your dog, but it is important to be consistent.

With Marty, say he is chasing a bird. I will tell him to "leave it," followed by "come." This is telling him to stop what he is doing, redirect his attention to me, and physically come to me. I am having him remove himself from the negative behavior he is exhibiting. Usually, when he comes to me, I will reward him with some play and redirect his attention. I'll have him

FAMOUS JRT'S
Frasier's Dogs

A pair of Jack Russell Terriers took turns playing Eddie Crane on the hit television sitcom Frasier, which aired from 1993 to 2004. Moose, Enzo's father, originally played Eddie. Enzo originally served as a stunt double as Moose aged, and the pair began alternating in the role during the eighth season of the show. Unfortunately, Moose passed away at the age of 15 on June 22, 2006, after enjoying six and a half years of retirement with trainer Mathilde de Cagny and her husband, Michael Halberg. Enzo, who also lived with Moose, passed away from cancer at the age of 14 on June 23, 2010.

Photo Courtesy of Roy "Digs" Degenstein Jr.

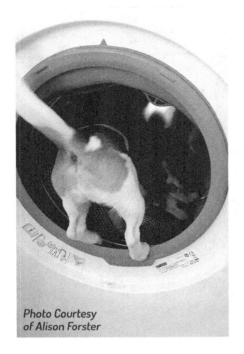

*Photo Courtesy
of Alison Forster*

sit in front of me and look at me, followed by a treat reward. Sometimes I will change directions completely and have him chase me down the path to get him completely distracted and excited about chasing me instead of the bird.

For your dog to fully comprehend what you are asking him, he will need to practice this every day. Make sure your positive interrupter is consistent and clear, follow up with an amazing treat after your positive interrupter, and teach your dog to disengage and to look at you (or come to you). Once your dog is solid on this, start practicing around distractions and things that are outside of your control, like that squirrel that runs across your path during your walk.

This is not a comprehensive list of methods to fix all bad habits, but it is a strong start for correcting most unwanted behaviors. Like I've said before, all dogs are different and respond differently to different training methods, but this one is tried and true to be effective with not only my own dog but other dogs I have trained and their owners.

Calling in a professional

Sometimes trying to correct a behavior can be overwhelming, or you feel like you have tried everything, and nothing seems to be working. Don't give up! Some behaviors take time and consistency to fix or require different methods. Sometimes, it has nothing to do with behavior and training, and there might actually be something going on medically with your dog.

Take peeing in the house, for example. This could be a demonstration of dominance, spite urination, separation anxiety, so on and so forth. However, this could also be a medical problem. This could be a urinary tract infection, an issue with incontinence, kidney issues, a whole lot of things; this is why it is a good idea to clue your veterinarian in on what behaviors you are seeing at home.

Photo Courtesy
of Wende Thompson

When you start the conversation with your veterinarian, he will want to know how long the behavior has been going on, when the behavior occurs, what happens before and after, how often it occurs, and what you have done so far to try to correct the behavior. Your veterinarian may want to do diagnostics, such as bloodwork, to see if there is anything medically occurring that may cause these behaviors.

CHAPTER FOURTEEN
Travel

> **"**
>
> *Jack Russells are the perfect size for traveling and usually travel very well. They take up little room in a car and can easily fit in a carry-on pet bag on a plane. Some Terriers handle car motion easily, while others require some practice. If your Terrier gets sick easily, work him up to traveling by taking him on short errands or to the park. Eventually, he will learn that the car leads someplace fun! Plane rides are made easier by getting the dog used to staying in a sherpa bag before travel. Put your JRT in there with treats and a chew stick and let him just hang out in the bag. Soon he will associate the bag with something good! While going through the airport, pay attention to your Terrier in the bag...some dogs like to see out, and others can't seem to handle all the stimulation. Take the dog's cue and close the privacy window if he seems reactive, or leave it open if he loves seeing all the commotion! Make sure you bring some snacks or chews and always reassure the dog that you are near!*
>
> ELLIE THOMPSON
> *Shavano Creek JRT*
>
> **"**

To bring your dog or not?

Traveling with your dog can be very challenging but can also be very rewarding. However, sometimes it is easier or more realistic to leave your dog behind, depending on the type of travel you are planning on doing. For me, Marty McFly came along for most of my travel, but sometimes I had to travel for work or attend a conference, and I had to make the choice to leave him with a sitter or at a kennel.

There are a lot of variables to consider when you are planning a trip and deciding whether or not your dog can come. I like to start by asking myself if my dog will benefit from coming with me or if the trip will actually give him and me more stress. Look at the type of trip you're planning. Is it a family event, a solo trip, or work-related? Sometimes that will help make the choice easier. Obviously, if you are going to be working all day or in meetings, your dog will be left in the hotel room unattended, which can be a liability. If you are planning a trip to national parks with the family, it can be challenging to bring a dog because most national parks prohibit dogs from being on trails, which will limit your experience. If you're planning a backpacking trip in the woods where the forest land allows dogs, that might be an awesome experience.

Photo Courtesy
of Donna Fugate

Whether or not you have decided to bring your dog with you or leave him behind, there are additional considerations that must be managed to give you peace of mind and to secure a fun and comfortable experience for your dog. If you are going to leave your dog behind, there are multiple options, such as having a pet sitter or boarding him at a kennel.

Leaving your dog home with a pet sitter

Leaving your dog with a pet sitter can mean a couple of different things. You have the option to let your dog stay with a friend or family member. A sitter can come to your home to take care of your house and your dog while you're gone. Or someone can come over multiple times a day to check in on the dog, feed him, and take him for walks. All of these are options, depending on the length of your trip and what would make your dog most comfortable.

Dropping your dog off at a sitter's house is one option. I have actually been a dog sitter for many dogs through word of mouth but also through applications such as the Rover app. In addition, I have left McFly at other people's homes while I was gone, and that worked well because he was comfortable with them. However, if someone said they would take him but were not going to be home, I got nervous because of his separation anxiety, and I didn't want him to annoy the neighbors with his barking. The best pet sitter I had for McFly was someone who was home on disability, so they spent the entire day with him, took him to the beach, and spoiled him rotten.

If you are going to leave your dog at someone's home, I recommend the person be someone you know and whose home you and your dog have visited before. This ensures you know the type of environment the dog will be in, such as if there are children, etc. If you decide to go with a company or an app, I encourage you to meet the person and their dog, if they have one, before you agree to have them pet sit for you. This will allow you to get a feel for the pet sitter, allow them to meet your dog, and allow you to see how your dog interacts with them. Ask questions about the person's home and what your dog's routine will look like. Many applications will require the sitter to send pictures and updates while you are on vacation, which is not only enjoyable but helps relieve some of the worry and stress.

The cost of leaving your dog in someone's home can vary widely depending on the person and the situation. Usually if it is a friend or family member, they will do it for free or for an exchange. It can be convenient if you both have dogs and can pet sit for one another. Otherwise, organizations or applications can charge anywhere between $25-$50 per day based on your location.

There is also the option of having someone come and stay in your home, which allows your dog to be in his own environment and makes sure your home is watched, and your plants are watered while you are gone. This was actually the first type of job I had as a teenager, and it was super enjoyable because it gave me freedom away from my family, and all I did was watch TV,

Photo Courtesy of Sally Herron

eat, and hang out with people's pets while getting paid. As an adult living in a beach town, this was also a great option because I could get people to come stay at my place for super cheap, and they got the benefit of being paid to stay at the beach while taking care of my home and dog. The downside was having someone get totally wasted and leave the house a mess, which I had to clean up when I returned home.

The cost is an agreement between you and the person staying in your home. Sometimes a fridge full of food is enough, and other times, especially if they are doing this as a job, the cost can range from $35-$75 a night. Again, this is variable, but most organizations or applications will list their pricings prior to your commitment.

One of the cheapest options is to just have someone come over a couple of times a day to walk and feed your dog. This can be fine for short trips, but for longer trips, it means your dog will spend a lot of time alone, which may cause more anxiety-based behaviors. Dogs are very social creatures and need attention. The cost for this kind of dog walking service would average between $10-$30 per day, and would be best for something like a quick weekend trip where you left Saturday morning and got back Sunday, so the time your dog spent alone would be minimized.

Leaving your dog at a kennel

Another good option is to leave your dog at a kennel or a dog hotel while you are away. There are a wide variety of boarding facilities, and I recommend visiting whichever one you are considering to see if you like it. Usually, these facilities will have a kennel designated for your dog, which can be anywhere from a weight and size-appropriate crate to a suite. Your dog will usually spend the majority of his time in a kennel, but he may also have an outside run where he can relieve himself as the kennel staff clean the sleeping area and prepare his food. Some facilities also have a group play location where multiple dogs will have an open space with toys and obstacles they can play around, in, and with. In addition, some places will allow you to add on walks or a bath.

The cost of boarding kennels can range from $25 to $85 a night, depending on the size of the accommodation. If you are going by weight, a Jack Russell Terrier will be cheaper than larger dogs, but if you decide to get a suite, it will be the same cost, no matter the size of the dog.

I recommend leaving your dog at a boarding facility for the day to see how he does. This allows you to start building a relationship with the staff and allows your dog to get conditioned to this new environment.

Boarding facilities have more requirements than leaving your dog with a pet sitter. You will have to show proof of your dog's vaccinations and will also have to get the Bordetella vaccine, which prevents kennel cough. Some facilities may also have additional requirements, such as flea and tick prevention. Any questions about requirements should be discussed with the boarding facility directly.

Photo Courtesy of Roy "Digs" Degenstein Jr

Taking your dog with you

> **"**
>
> *I always recommend a secure crate whenever possible. It is safest for the dog and for the driver. Always make sure to have identification on your dog when traveling, and make sure your dog has a microchip. Make certain the collar or harness is securely fitted so the dog cannot slip out when walking in strange places and/or close to roads. Use a secure leash and not a retractable one. Always watch for hazards in the grass and in new places that might draw your dog's interest. If you choose not to use a crate for travel, try to at least secure the dog in the vehicle when traveling long distances.*
>
> WENDY PALMER
> *Thistle Ridge Terriers*
>
> **"**

Bringing your dog with you on a trip is an awesome way to increase the bond you have with him. That said, traveling with your dog can be very challenging, especially if there are limited pet-friendly places and activities. Pet-friendly means that the company, organization, or place allows pets, usually dogs, to be in the location. This includes bars, restaurants, parks, and places to stay. If you are traveling with your dog, you should start planning your trip by looking at pet-friendly places around the place you are going.

Dog-friendly stays

Some of the most pet-friendly places are camping-based. Camping and dogs tend to go hand in hand, but you want to make sure you follow the campsite rules and regulations. Usually, rabies vaccines are required, and all dogs need to be on a leash. Campsites are great because they are family-friendly, and you can find locations where there is running water, toilets, and showers, or you can find campsites that are off-grid, where there is only a designated spot to pitch your tent, and if you're lucky, a firepit. Lots of campsites are located next to trails or water features like a river or a lake, which gives you even more opportunity to explore with your dog.

Camping can be a relatively cost-effective way to travel and take your dog on a trip. Usually a campsite costs between $7-$35 a night, depending on location and amenities.

If camping isn't your jam and you would prefer a roof over your head, there are a lot of pet-friendly hotel chains, and even Airbnb has dog-friendly places you can enjoy. When looking at a pet-friendly hotel, check the fine print to see if they have any pet fees. If they do, they usually range from $20-$40. Note that lots of hotels will have a limit of two dogs max and a weight limit of 80 pounds, but this varies by location. Some locations, such as the Four Seasons, have no pet fee and will include a luxury pet bed, treats, and bowls filled with Evian water. Some hotels may even offer additional amenities, such as a dog-friendly menu or dog walks for an extra charge.

On the Airbnb website, there isn't a specific filter that can show you all the pet-friendly stays, but it is usually listed in the description. If you are unsure, message the host and tell them about your dog, and see what they say. The benefit of having a Jack Russell is that they are a smaller breed, which makes hosts feel better. I usually let the host know that my dog will never be left alone because he will be out exploring with me.

Dog-friendly locations, places, and activities

When planning a trip, it is also great to do a Google search to see what locations, places, and activities are dog-friendly. This can depend on the state and the city you are in. Some places may list themselves as pet-friendly or dog-friendly, but this may come with specific rules; for example, a restaurant may be dog-friendly, but that could mean that dogs are only allowed out on the patio and can't come inside.

A lot of breweries and bars tend to be a bit more pet-friendly because many don't have a kitchen, so they aren't preparing food, which is the number one reason animals aren't allowed inside restaurants. Make sure to call ahead or check the website of a location to see what their specific policies are. When going to these locations, make sure your dog is fully vaccinated, has a bowl for water, and has a sturdy leash just in case he gets overly excited.

When planning dog-friendly activities, be attentive to outdoor spaces and nature-based adventures. Though it would seem natural that dogs are allowed to go on nature trails, a lot of trails don't allow dogs due to preservation. Every trailhead and park should have a posting on whether dogs are allowed and what the regulations are. Usually, all trails and parks require dogs to be on a six-foot leash. National parks, as mentioned before, do not allow dogs. That being said, some parks will have one or two dog-friendly trails, but do not plan on this, and make sure to check before you go.

Beaches are another outdoor space that can vary when it comes to whether dogs are allowed or not. Some places will have dog-specific beaches. Again, there should be something posted stating whether dogs are allowed and if they need to be on a leash. For all outdoor spaces, please don't forget to clean up after your pet and dispose of poop in a bag in the designated trash receptacles.

Traveling in the car

Some dogs take to the car and car travel very well, while others have a difficult time with it. Getting your dog used to riding in the car is very beneficial. Some people only put their dog in the car when he is going to the veterinarian. If the dog only gets in the car to go to a stressful experience, he will start to associate the car with negativity, and anxiety will ensue. However, there are ways to mitigate this from occurring, and the first step is to manage expectations for your dog when he is riding in the car.

The car can be a dangerous place for anyone but is especially dangerous for your dog. If he is unrestrained in the car, he can sustain a multitude of injuries if you have to brake quickly, get hit by another vehicle, or if you open the door and he jumps out unexpectedly. Any of these situations can be dangerous and can happen without warning. Here are some expectations and car safety rules I highly recommend.

Always restrain your dog.

Photo Courtesy of Marne Yarbrough

For long-distance trips, I recommend putting your dog in a crate so he has an extra layer of protection. For short-distance trips, like errands, I recommend getting a doggie seat belt, and for Jack Russell Terriers, I recommend a car bed that has a seat-belt attachment that also attaches to your dog. This prevents your dog from being tossed around and dramatically reduces the probability of a severe injury. When restraining your dog, always, always, always use a harness and not a collar. A dog restrained only by the collar is at increased risk of severe injury or death in a motor vehicle collision.

Expect him to wait in the car until you release him to get out.

This is another serious safety concern. Your dog should wait every single time the door is opened until you have detached him from the car seat belt and have him attached to the regular leash. Only when you say it is okay for him to get out of the car can he do so. I have had some owners come into the clinic as an emergency because their dog jumped out of their car and got hit by another car in a parking lot. Make sure you solidify this expectation for your dog to wait. I don't care how excited he gets at the dog park; he has to wait until otherwise directed. End of story.

Make sure he is comfortable in the car through desensitization.

If your dog has car anxiety or is unfamiliar with cars, I recommend letting him hang out in the car when you aren't going anywhere. If I am working in the garage, I will open up the car door, put my dog in there with a chew toy or a treat feeder and let him just hang out in there. Some dogs I have fostered have had severe car anxiety, so I will sit in the car with them, have lunch or clean the car out so the dog can get used to the car being as familiar as the couch in the living room.

Once your dog seems desensitized a bit, take him for short rides around the neighborhood or to cool places that are positive reinforcers for him, such as a park or Home Depot. Allow him to have a fun break before getting back into the car and going home. Also, if you are ever at the veterinarian, whether picking up preventative meds, dog food, or dropping goodies off for the staff, bring your dog with you. This helps him realize that going to the vet doesn't always mean he is going to get poked.

Give your dog his space in the car.

This ties to the safety measures mentioned before, but this also gives your dog some routine. Every time he gets in the car, he knows he needs to lie down in the kennel or stay in his bed. This provides structure for him and a familiar place, just like the dog crate in the house.

Traveling by plane

Traveling with your dog on a plane seems to be getting more and more difficult each year. Luckily, being a Jack Russell owner, you will be able to take your dog with you in the aircraft cabin itself due to the dog's small size. It is important to look at which airlines accept dogs in the cabin and what their restrictions are. Here are some universal standards required for traveling by airplane.

- **Health certificate:** Most airlines require you to go to a veterinarian and obtain a health certificate within seven to 10 days of traveling by plane. Not all veterinarians can do this, so it is best to call your veterinary clinic prior to travel to see if it can provide this service.

- **Make sure your dog is up to date on vaccinations:** Most airlines are concerned about the rabies vaccine because rabies is a public health concern, and you will need a rabies certificate or proof of rabies vaccination. Other vaccines may be recommended but are not always required. Check with the specific airline you are traveling with.

FUN FACT

Parson Russell vs. Jack Russell

Parson Russell Terriers and Jack Russell Terriers have a long-shared history and were only recently recognized as independent breeds. Parson Russells are typically slightly taller at 13–14 inches, weigh between 13–17 pounds, and usually have a squarer body and broader chest. Jack Russells generally are 10–12 inches and weigh around 9–15 pounds.

- **A crate:** Crates are required for all dogs who are traveling, and if your dog will be traveling in the cabin with you, the crate will need to fit under the seat in front of you and counts as your personal item. Ideally, your dog should be able to stand, turn, and lie down. I personally always fly with Marty in a soft crate so he can have more flexibility when he lies down, and the crate tends to be lighter overall. A simple search on Amazon for "airplane-friendly dog carrier" will get you all the examples you need.

- **Identification:** Having a collar or harness with your dog's tags is great, just in case you get separated from your dog. In addition to identification tags, also consider getting a microchip for your dog, which will provide him with a permanent form of identification, even if he has lost his collar.

Traveling by train, bus, or boat

There are not a lot of other modes of transportation that allow dogs. Buses only allow service dogs, and Amtrak trains allow dogs who are under

20 pounds—again great news for us Jack Russell owners. Some boats and ferries allow dogs but have specific requirements. New York City, for example, requires a muzzle on your dog when traveling by ferry, and on the metro train system, your dog has to fit within a bag.

Tips and tricks for a successful trip

> *Traveling with small breeds is very easy. A safe crate is needed with enough space to move about and be comfortable. It is never recommended to have a dog loose in a vehicle while driving. It could distract you, or the dog could become injured or lost if you have an accident. If your dog is reactive or aggressive to others, be aware and respectful. Give your dog the space and privacy he wants and needs. For example, if you stop at a hotel, check in without your dog first. If you stop at a rest area, park far enough away so that your dog can potty in peace.*
>
> **GINA E. SNOW**
> *Swanback Jacks*

 **TIP 01** When traveling, it is helpful to plan out bathroom breaks and make sure your dog is comfortable relieving himself on different surface types.

 **TIP 02** Make sure you have plenty of bags to clean up after your dog.

 **TIP 03** Bring entertainment for your dog in the form of toys and chews. I personally love bringing puzzle toys to make sure McFly doesn't get bored.

 **TIP 04** Pack food and water, especially if your dog is on a special diet. Travel can cause stress, and there is no need to double that stress by dramatically changing your dog's food.

 **TIP 05** If bringing your dog on a long trip or vacation, make sure you look into dog-friendly places to stay, restaurants, and places to take him.

CHAPTER FIFTEEN
Nutrition

Choosing the appropriate diet for your dog

> "
>
> *Choosing a diet appropriate for your dog's activity level is very important. Choose a high-quality, balanced food. Pay special attention to dental health. Make certain the dog's nails stay trimmed. An active dog can easily stay fit well into his older years, so make sure exercise is a big part of his life. And don't overfeed him or give him too many treats. Most Jack Russells are just as happy to have a toy as a reward as a snack, so make healthy rewards a priority.*
>
> WENDY PALMER
> *Thistle Ridge Terriers*
>
> "

Dog food is one of the most controversial topics in the canine world. There are some people who feel strongly about what they believe is best for their dogs. The most important opinion that should be considered is that of your veterinarian. Vets have years of training and a deep understanding of what your dog needs, how much food he should be fed, and what kind of diet would be best for your dog. Note also that your dog's diet will change at different life stages.

Dog food is highly regulated, and the quality of commercial dog food undergoes rigorous testing by veterinary specialists. That is why recalls, although scary, are actually good because it shows the commitment and regulation of that dog food company. Dogs are not strict carnivores and can gain nutritional benefits from a variety of foods, including fruits, vegetables, and grains. When looking at dog food, look at the labels and see if there are a variety of nutrient sources. Good dog food will have not only meat and grains but also fruit and vegetables.

Some people have questions about animal by-products. Animal by-products is just an umbrella name for organ meats and entrails. When the food industry processes food for human consumption, there isn't a large market for these types of meats, so many dog food companies use these meats, which is great because organ meat has a lot of nutrients.

There are also grain-free, pea-free, or limited ingredient diets. These diets are usually recommended by a veterinarian if your dog has allergies, especially those allergies caused by grains. A grain free diet has become popular in recent years and many dog owners have switched their dogs to a grain free diet, however, grains are actually an important nutritional source for dogs. If a grain-free or limited ingredient diet is not recommended by the veterinarian for your dog, it is best to choose another type of diet.

It is important to read the food label on your dog's food. There could be a whole book just written on the dog food industry, and the Merck Veterinary Manual is a very good resource if you would like to deep dive into the subject. All dog food labels must contain a product name, net weight of the product, name and address of the manufacturer, guaranteed analysis, list of ingredients, intended animal species, statement of nutritional adequacy, and feeding guidelines. The Food and Drug Administration (FDA) requires that these things be listed on all dog food bags.

Photo Courtesy of Rebecca & Gabe Morales

When looking into dog food, remember a Jack Russell will need a slightly different diet than, say, a Newfoundland. Jack Russell Terriers are not as prone to musculoskeletal problems as larger dogs and also may not be able to eat larger-sized kibble. A dog food that is small-breed specific is advisable for a Jack Russell, but it is also good to talk to your veterinarian about any food recommendations he may have specifically for your dog.

When choosing a dog food, it is important to consider a dog food that will provide the greatest nutritional value for the health of your dog. This depends on your dog's activity level, age, and size. Some dogs have food allergies that can limit the types of dog food they can have, and some dogs can be picky about taste. Lastly, your lifestyle also matters, and it is important to look at the amount of time you do or don't have to shop and cook meals for your dog.

Kibble

Dry dog food kibble is the most common type of dog food because it has a longer shelf life, is easier to produce, and is easier to store. Kibble can help prevent plaque buildup because of the abrasiveness of the food, which helps clean the teeth and promote healthier gums. There is a reduced risk of bacteria because it has already been cooked. However, there are a large number of dry dog food manufactures and practices, so it is important to look at the ingredients themselves.

All dry dog food kibble is required to have a source of protein, such as beef, poultry, fish, and eggs; kibble must contain grains or cereals, as well as vitamins, minerals, and antioxidants. However, some dog food companies may not use the highest-quality ingredients and may use more fillers to bulk up the food, reducing its nutritional value. When looking at dry dog food kibble labels, look to see if a grain or a protein is the first ingredient. You want to see a protein there, ideally a single-source protein, such as lamb or chicken. Grains are still an essential source of energy for your dog. You just don't want them listed as the main ingredient.

Personally, I like dry dog food kibble because it helps with maintaining a dog's teeth; it is convenient, financially feasible, and you can use it for food enrichment such as food puzzles or slow feeders. When looking into dry dog food kibble brands, look at the label, and feel free to research the company, but also ask for your veterinarian's recommendation. The most common dry food recommendations are Royal Canin and Science Diet.

Wet food

Wet food is very similar to dry dog kibble, but instead of being turned into a dough, cooked, and shaped into kibble, it is cooked with gravy and canned. This type of processing helps it maintain higher moisture content, which may be beneficial for some dogs. Some dogs need a higher moisture diet because they don't drink enough water on their own, or they may have kidney disease or urinary issues. Canned dog food is more palatable to dogs because it is more aromatic and flavorful, which might entice picky eaters, especially if a dog is sick or old. Wet food also provides more satiety, allowing a dog to feel full longer, which might be helpful in dogs with weight management issues. A wet diet is easier to chew for dogs that have severe dental problems.

A lot of people regularly give their dogs both dry food and canned food. This allows you to give your dog the best of both worlds. If you leave your dog in the morning when you go to work, I recommend giving him his wet food in the morning so that he feels full longer and has added moisture when he may be less likely to drink. Make sure if you do choose to feed your dog both wet and dry food, that you discuss with your vet your dog's daily caloric needs to prevent overfeeding.

Raw food

Make sure to feed your Terrier the best food you can. Research kibble for ingredients and recall histories. Know what you are feeding your Terrier and why. Know what his stools look like, so when he's not feeling well, you will know. Many families like to feed raw or cooked diets, so they have more control over ingredients. Whatever you choose, please do your research and find out what your Terrier is eating! Needless to say, lots of love and cuddles also help any Terrier stay healthy!

ELLIE THOMPSON
Shavano Creek JRT

Raw food diets tend to be highly controversial, and there are very strong opinions on both sides. The diet focuses on feeding your dog raw meat, bones, fruits, and vegetables. This diet is based on what dogs ate before they became domesticated. There are also a few offshoots of the raw diet, which include frozen raw and freeze-dried diets that have been commercially processed with some grains, vegetables, and vitamins.

The raw food diet claims to provide healthier skin, shinier coats, cleaner teeth, higher energy levels, and smaller stools, but the potential for bacterial contamination, a dog choking on a bone, breaking a tooth, or having an intestinal rupture makes the diet very risky. In addition, many raw food diets have been researched and tested, and all have fallen short of being able to provide a balanced diet for dogs, which can lead to long-term health issues if a dog is fed a raw food diet for a long time, especially during the developmental stages of a canine's life. If you feel strongly about making your dog's food, it is recommended that you consult a veterinary nutritionist.

Photo Courtesy
of Nina Chang and Brook Lloyd

Homemade food

Homemade food is made with natural ingredients such as beef, chicken, lamb, peas, carrots, spinach, blueberries, and sweet potatoes cooked in a stew or a mash. This diet can lead to the promotion of heart health, increased energy levels, healthier coats, and can impact gut health. However, cooking homemade meals for your dog can not only be time-consuming and put a dent in your finances, but it can also lead to vitamin and nutrition imbalances if not done with guidance from a veterinarian. If you decide you want to pursue this type of diet, you may also need to add supplementation to your dog's diet under the guidance of your veterinarian. It may also be beneficial to consider incorporating a mixture of a homemade diet with some canned or dry kibble in order to increase the probability of providing your dog with a balanced diet.

No matter what diet you choose, it is important to provide the nutrition your dog needs for the specific stage of life he is in. Puppies grow rapidly, and they need a diet that supports this rapid growth. Once a puppy starts to eat dog food, meaning he is no longer relying on mother's milk, he will need to eat a diet that is specifically formulated for growing puppies until they are 12

months old. Larger-breed dogs may need to be on this diet until they are 18 months old.

Once your Jack Russell has reached a year of age, you can gradually transition him over to an adult diet. This diet will have slightly fewer calories, and the nutrients, minerals, and vitamins may change slightly because the diet is no longer supporting growth but is more for maintenance. Adult diets usually start at one year of age and go to about five to seven years; Jack Russell Terriers will probably be at the higher end of that range.

FAMOUS JRT'S
Chalky

Chalky was a Jack Russell Terrier and companion to English celebrity chef Rick Stein. Chalky was born in August 1989 and was a near-constant presence on Stein's popular cooking shows. The Jack Russell Terrier became so well-known that a line of merchandise featuring his likeness was produced, as well as two beers, Chalky's Bite and Chalky's Bark. Unfortunately, Chalky passed away in January 2007.

Once your dog has reached seven to eight years of age, your veterinarian may recommend switching him to a senior diet, which will have fewer calories but will have more supplements, vitamins, and minerals like omega-3s or fish oil to support an aging dog's body.

Before you switch your dog's diet, especially if you are considering going to a different life stage formula, you should talk to your veterinarian. They know your dog best, they understand where their metabolic and nutritional needs lie, and they can give you the best guidance on how and when to switch.

Marty McFly has gone through a lot of different diets. When he was a puppy, we started on an age-specific diet for puppies, which tends to have higher protein to support a growing body. Then, when he became an adult, we switched him to a small-dog adult diet. The actual types of diet changed based on what veterinary clinic I was working at and what type of food we kept in-house. Hill's is often what I chose because of this. Once McFly became a senior, seven-plus years old, we switched to a senior diet. Unfortunately, last year he was diagnosed with kidney disease, so he is now on a kidney diet that was prescribed by his veterinarian.

Treat recipes to make at home

I love to make dog treats at home for Marty McFly, but I also love to give treats as gifts to all my friends with dogs. Most dog treat recipes can be pretty easy to make, and dogs tend to be an easy crowd to please. Dog treat recipes are very similar to human cookies, but instead of sugar, it is recommended to use blackstrap molasses, and carob is a solid replacement for chocolate.

I personally try to use the simplest and most natural ingredients when I am making my dog treats. If I'm using peanut butter, for example, I try to get versions that have no sugar added and that have the least amount of ingredients. When looking at no sugar added, make sure there aren't artificial sweeteners that can potentially be toxic. For example, xylitol is an artificial sweetener that can be life-threatening to dogs. DOGBUTTER is a peanut butter made specifically for dogs.

Peanut Butter Gingerbread Dog Treats

3 cups all-purpose flour

1 tsp. baking soda for soft treats (for hard treats, you can leave this out)

1 tsp. ground cinnamon

1 tsp. ground cloves

1 tbsp ginger paste or 1 tsp. of ginger powder

1/3 cup peanut butter

1 egg

1 tsp. vanilla

3/4 cup of water

Instructions:

Preheat the oven to 325 degrees Fahrenheit, and line a baking sheet with parchment paper.

In a large bowl, mix all the dry ingredients together—flour, baking soda, cinnamon, cloves, and ginger if using the powdered ginger. If you are using ginger paste, add it to the wet mix. Make a divot or large impression in the center of the wet mixture. Set aside.

In a smaller bowl, mix all of your wet ingredients—egg, peanut butter, molasses, water, and vanilla. Once these ingredients are whisked together, add to the impression in your dry mix and stir together.

Lightly dust your work surface with flour and roll out your dough into a 1/4-inch thick sheet. You can cut the cookies into small squares or use your favorite cookie cutter shape.

Lay out the dough onto your parchment-lined cookie sheet and pierce the center of the cookies for heat release. This is the time to get creative and make a gingerbread person design, such as buttons. Bake for 10–12 minutes, or until the cookie bottoms become golden brown. Remove cookies from the oven and place them on a cooling rack. They will continue to harden up during the cooling process, so make sure not to overcook!

Pumpkin Butter Dog Bones

2/3 cup pumpkin puree (*do not use pumpkin pie filling!)

1/4 cup peanut butter

2 large eggs

3 cups whole wheat flour

Instructions:

Preheat oven to 350 degrees Fahrenheit, and line a baking sheet with parchment paper.

Mix pumpkin puree, peanut butter, and eggs together in a bowl. You can whisk this, but it is best to use an electric mixer. Mix for 1–2 minutes or until well combined, then gradually add the flour to the mixture. Mix in the dough until it is no longer sticky to the touch.

Lightly flour your work surface and knead the dough 3–4 times or until it starts to come together. Roll out the dough until it is about 1/4-inch thick. Use a dog-bone-shaped cookie cutter to cut out your cookies and place them on the parchment-lined baking sheet.

Place in oven and cook for 20–25 minutes or until the edges become golden brown. Remove and let cool on a wire rack before serving.

This last recipe is super simple and is a great jumping-off point for anyone who would like to experiment with baking dog treats. You can easily replace the pumpkin with sweet potato puree or replace some of the flour with rolled oats, for example. Be creative, but always research your ingredients first to make sure you are only using dog-friendly food!

Foods to keep your dog away from

There are a variety of different foods that can upset a dog's stomach, but there are also a variety of foods that can be very toxic to them and can even cause death. Here is a list of the most common foods that dogs should never eat. If your dog has eaten something that you are unsure about, call your veterinarian or go to the Pet Poison Helpline (www.petpoisonhelpline. com)website.

The top ten most common toxic foods for dogs are:

1. Chocolate

2. Xylitol (found in sugar-free gum and other foods)

3. Grapes and raisins

4. Onions and garlic

5. Apple seeds and fruit pits

6. Coffee (grounds, beans, and chocolate-covered espresso beans)

7. Alcohol

8. Macadamia nuts and walnuts

9. Leaves and stems of potatoes and tomatoes

10. Yeast dough (it causes stomach expansion)

Weight management

Managing your Jack Russell's weight is very important for his health and longevity. If your Jack Russell is not getting enough nutrition, he will be in a deficit, which can lead not only to health issues but behavioral issues as well. On the other hand, feeding your Jack Russell too much can impact his musculoskeletal and cardiovascular systems, as well as have other health implications.

A good weight for these dogs is hard to define because Jack Russell Terriers can vary slightly in size and build. A good guideline is that you should be able to see a slight outline of the ribs, a waist, and be able to feel the hip bones. If the ribs are prominent and the hip bones are jutting out, the dog is probably too skinny. If you can't really see the ribs, there is a minimal to no waist, and you have trouble finding the hip bones, the dog is probably too heavy. If you are in doubt, ask your veterinarian for guidance.

Personally, I found that managing McFly's weight has been relatively easy. Yes, he did go through his skinny and chubby phases, but he is so small that a minor alteration to the amount of food I feed him can cause drastic results. I make sure to pay attention to his weight at vet visits to see if there have been any extreme changes over time. Weight loss recently, in his case, was one of the indicators that something was wrong with him. The weight loss, among other signs and symptoms, led us to the diagnosis of kidney disease. Any extreme change to your dog's weight that cannot be linked to changes in feeding habits should be addressed by your veterinarian. Dogs, like humans, can get thyroid disease or other metabolic diseases that can present as drastic weight changes.

CHAPTER SIXTEEN
Grooming

Different types of Jack Russell coats

> *Jack Russells have three main coats: smooth, broken, and rough. No matter which you have, there are several layers to the coat, and shaving a dog's coat is not always best. Smooth Terriers may seem easy to maintain; however, they shed FAR more than their broken or rough relatives! We keep Roombas on each floor of our home for this specific purpose! Broken and rough-coat Terriers require a little more upkeep. A good stripping knife is key to keeping them tidy. Hand stripping the fur and rolling the coat is the traditional method of keeping JRTs looking tidy but can take time to learn. A SleekEZ brush can keep the dog looking nice in between groomings and will remove stray hairs from the undercoat. If grooming a Terrier is not something you care to learn, look for a groomer who understands a Terrier's coat and how to care for it. No matter the coat, always keep the dog's toenails clipped and his teeth brushed. We sometimes use a human electric brush to keep our dogs' teeth clean! Not every Terrier is thrilled with this idea, though!*
>
> ELLIE THOMPSON
> *Shavano Creek JRT*

Jack Russell Terriers have three different types of coats: smooth, broken, and rough. All three are double coats where the hair is relatively flat and hardy to repel dirt and plant matter.

The **smooth coat** of the Jack Russell is consistently short around the face, body, and legs but is still coarse. This is probably the easiest of the three coats to take care of because many elements slide right off it.

A **rough coat** will have slightly longer hair than a smooth coat, and the hair, though still coarse, will be wiry and straight, growing in a variety of directions, giving them a more textured look. This coat may be slightly more challenging while grooming, and the rough-coated Jack Russell may need some trimming around the face.

A **broken coat** is a combination of a smooth and a rough coat, giving them a few areas of longer fur and variety throughout their fur. This doesn't require additional grooming and still helps protect them from the elements.

Bathing and brushing

Jack Russell Terriers can be bathed every 4-6 weeks at a maximum. They are pretty clean dogs and have coats that repel a lot of dirt. If your Jack Russell is visibly dirty or smelly, you can bathe them more often. Sometimes a good rinse with clean water will do the trick.

Before bathing, it is good to familiarize your dog with the process of bathing and the location of the bath itself. Many people bathe their dog in the bathtub because it is where we bathe ourselves, and it is the traditional spot most people associate with bathing a dog. If this is where you are comfortable with bathing your dog, desensitize them to this area. You can bring them into a dry bathtub with you in it and hang out with them in there. Practice their sit and stay commands in there, as you will probably need to use them during your bath.

Another great spot to bathe your Jack Russell is in a sink. I personally don't mind bathing them in the kitchen sink for routine baths because I will do it before I do a deep clean of the kitchen, so any hair or grim left over will be cleaned up anyway. Another option is in a garage sink or in a tub outside. Whatever you choose, you can desensitize your dog by putting them in it, giving them treats, asking for a sit, and praising them.

When you feel like you and your dog are ready for their bath, make sure to collect all the materials you need before you start. Have a towel on the floor near you, another towel within quick reach, shampoo, and a bath brush if you choose to use one. I also recommend having a couple of treats nearby to give them positive reinforcement for being good. Make sure to use a dog-specific shampoo when bathing your dog. If you don't have one available and your dog needs a bath urgently, aka rolled in poop, you can use dawn dish soap, but this is not recommended for routine use.

When bathing your Jack Russell, make sure to wet them down from the back of the ears

HELPFUL TIP
Choosing a Brush

All three Jack Russell Coat types—smooth, broken, and rough—are high shedding, so regular brushing is a must with this breed. A slicker brush is a great all-around brush for Jack Russell Terriers for removing fur and preventing mats. Some Jack Russell owners also use a shedding rake to remove loose hair, but excessive use of this type of brush can cause irritation. A rubber brush glove or rubber brush are great tools for gently removing loose hair from your dog's coat, as well as your furniture!

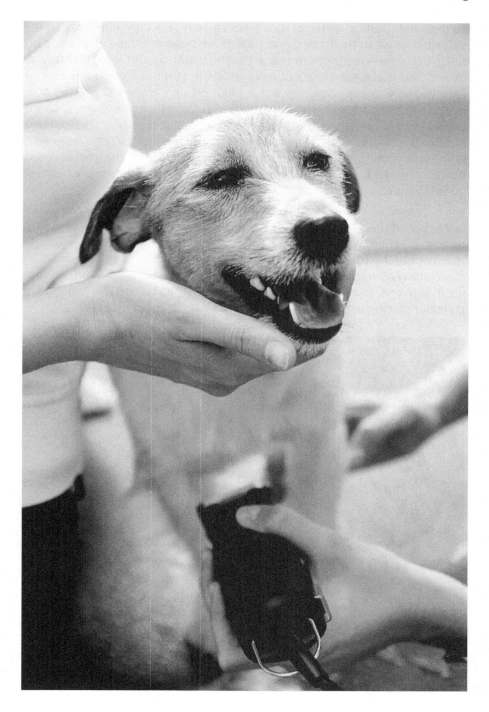

to their tail. Getting water in their ears can cause an ear infection, so it is safer to not wash their head and face. If the head and face of the dog are dirty, use a wet washcloth in this area. The water should feel good to your touch, and make sure it is not too hot. Once you have soaked their coat with water, you can apply the soap. Most often, people will put the soap just along the back of their dog and then rub it in, but the back is one of the least common areas that they are going to get dirty and smelly. I usually put the shampoo in my hands and rub the neck, chest, and belly area. Once you have fully scrubbed and cleaned their coat, rinse the soap out thoroughly. To help in this, remember that a small amount of shampoo goes a long way.

Before trying to dry your Jack Russell, try and squeeze any remaining water out of their coat with your hands. Then, while they are still in the tub or sink, dry them with their towel. Once they are no longer soaking wet, take them out of the tub and allow them to run around. Jack Russell Terriers are particularly adorable after a bath because they love to run around, roll, and dig in blankets, towels, or their bed in order to get dry. Keep this in mind and consider placing extra towels on their bed.

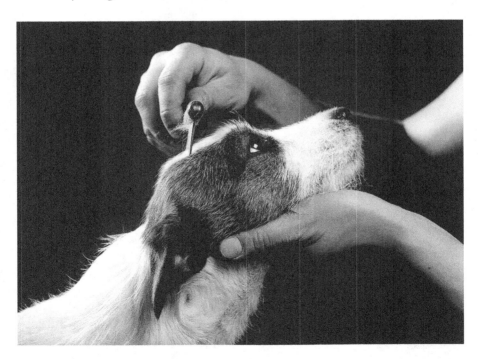

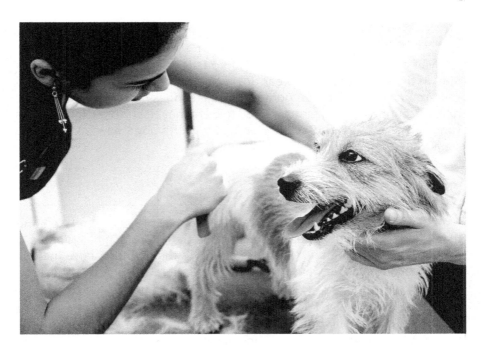

If your dog has just rolled in something disgusting, rinse that out thoroughly before you do your bath. You may also need to wash them multiple times to get the smell out, depending on how bad it is. Try to prevent using shampoo with a lot of perfume in it, even if you are tempted. You can use dawn dish soap first to get rid of the majority of the disgusting smell and/or material, and then use your regular dog shampoo right after.

A brushing before and after a bath is recommended. The brushing before will help mitigate any loose hairs or potential matting that has built up over the past couple of weeks. The brushing after the bath will help collect the hair that was loosened during the bath.

I routinely brush McFly once a week in order to try and mitigate the amount of hair he sheds in the house. I use a Furminator to pull up a lot of his undercoat, and I feel that it helps.

I probably bathe McFly once a month with a dog-friendly shampoo, which is a little more often than average. Usually, dogs need to be bathed every two to three months, but McFly and I often go to the beach and kayak in the bay, so he is interacting with a variety of stinky environments, which are also very salty, so he can get pretty smelly very quickly.

Nail care

Nail care is an important part of your Jack Russell's grooming routine. In the wild, dogs' nails wear down due to rough terrain, digging, and self-grooming behaviors. In domesticated life, dogs don't wear down their nails as routinely, and their nails need to be managed. If left neglected, nails can grow long, curl, and actually embed into the dog's paw pad, causing significant damage and difficulty walking.

Clipping your dog's nails

When clipping your dog's nails, make sure he is calm and relaxed and that you have everything ready and at hand. Gather up dog nail clippers, a towel, styptic powder, and lots of treats. Sit on the floor and have the dog come over and sit in between your legs. Give him a few treats and some love.

Next, get the dog into a lying position either on his side or his back, depending on the dog and what he will tolerate. Sometimes for smaller dogs like Jack Russell Terriers, I will sit them on my lap and then bring them up on their hind legs with their back against my chest and arm, restraining them that way. It just depends on the dog.

Talk soothingly and sweetly to the dog, and then clip the first nail. Follow this up immediately with a praise and a treat. Then continue onto the next nail and repeat the praise and treat. Once the dog gets more used to it, give a treat every two or three nails to make the process go a little faster. If, for some reason, you clip a nail too close and it starts to bleed, use styptic powder to stop the bleed. Sometimes clipping a dog's nails can be made easier by wrapping him in a towel like you would a baby.

I personally like the scissor-type nail clippers because you have more control, and they don't break the nails as much as guillotine-style clippers. Dremel has a dog-specific grinder that can also grind down your dog's nails, but I find that grinders are loud, and many dogs don't like the sound or the feel of them. However, they are very good at rounding out the nail tips so that they are smooth and don't scratch as much. Styptic powder is specially formulated for clipped nails in dogs and can be purchased at your local pet store, but if you don't have any at home, cornstarch will work just fine.

I take nail care seriously and trim McFly's nails once a week. He and I have a good understanding of the expectations when it comes to me trimming his nails. I often sit on the back porch and flip him onto his back, lying on my legs. When I clip his nails, I usually start with the white or clear toenails because I can see the pink nerve ending, called the quick. This is a good guide to how far back I can cut without hitting the quick and causing bleeding.

Some dogs may not need to have their nails cut every week; it just depends on what activities they are doing that may naturally wear their nails down. When we moved to the city, McFly's nails would need less trimming because we walked on sidewalks. When I have a busy week or two and am unable to walk him as much, I can see a difference.

Dental care

Dental care is a major contributor to the health of your dog. Poor dental health can lead to pain in the mouth, trouble eating, gum disease, and issues with the organs and cardiovascular system. Your dog's dental care will take a combined effort between yourself and your veterinarian. At home, you can help prevent plaque build-up and periodontal disease by giving your dog dental-specific chews, brushing his teeth regularly, and watching for any changes in the mouth such as broken teeth or unusual growths. Make sure to use dog-specific toothpaste because some ingredients in human toothpaste can be toxic to dogs. It may take some time to get your dog desensitized and used to brushing, so I recommend starting this at a very young age.

Brushing your dog's teeth

When starting to incorporate tooth brushing into your dog's routine, wait until he is calm and relaxed and pick a time that works best for you. Right when you come home is probably not advisable given that your dog is probably super excited to see you, and you may be tired from your day. Maybe consider it as part of your bedtime routine; after you brush your teeth, you may want to brush your dog's. For puppies, you don't have to do the entire mouth; start with just the front teeth, the incisors, and then the next day do the top right-hand side, the next day the bottom, so on and so forth.

You will want to use a toothbrush made for dogs, and you can probably get away with a finger toothbrush for your Jack Russell Terrier because their mouths are so small. Make sure you have dog-friendly toothpaste, and I usually keep a hand towel nearby for additional cleanup. Get down to your dog's level, allow him to smell the toothpaste, and then try to rub it on his front teeth to get started. Dog toothpaste usually comes in tasty flavors, so your dog will try to lick it while you brush, and that is okay.

Finger toothbrushes are nice because they fit right over your finger, and you have a lot more control over them. Rub your finger with the toothpaste along the dog's gums and teeth in small sections. Again, this may take some

*Photo Courtesy
of Nina Chang and Brooke Lloyd*

time for the dog to get used to, but practice every day, and he will become more and more comfortable with this weird routine. Eventually, you will want to be able to do the entire mouth, just like you do for yourself.

Use a circular motion. Make sure to get those hard-to-reach back teeth and do the inside and outside of the teeth. If you are using a toothbrush, make sure that you use it at a 45-degree angle and also make sure not to use too much pressure and cause gum damage. Blood is common, especially if you are inconsistent with brushing, but at any point, if you think it is excessive, talk to your veterinarian.

Your veterinarian will conduct an oral exam during your dog's physical to see if there is a need for a dental cleaning. Dogs don't sit nicely and open their mouths for your veterinarian to poke around in, so your Jack Russell will need to be placed under anesthesia for a dental cleaning and/or procedure. This will usually require some blood work prior to the procedure to check for any underlying issues that may complicate the anesthesia.

On the day of your dog's dental procedure, you will need to drop him off for the procedure, and some paperwork will need to be signed. Once your dog is anesthetized, the veterinary staff will clean your dog's teeth by scaling them. An ultrasonic scaler uses a combination of vibration and water to get between the plaque and tarter. It also allows the veterinary staff to reach the tarter below the gum line, which can cause significant periodontal disease. If there are any teeth that are a cause for worry, they may take some X-rays to look at the tooth as a whole, including its nerve root under the gum. If extractions are needed, your veterinarian will take your dog's tooth or teeth out and then suture up the gums if needed. Then the rest of the teeth will be polished, much like your dentist would do for your mouth. This procedure may vary slightly from clinic to clinic, but essentially, the process is the same.

Periodontal disease is the most common dental issue in dogs, and it usually starts manifesting around three years of age. The disease will progress and cause serious issues down the line if preventative measures are not taken. Usually, periodontal disease starts as plaque that hardens into tartar. It is easy to see this tartar because it is happening above the gum line, but plaque and tartar under the gum line can lead to infection in the connective tissues and the jawbone itself. By maintaining your dog's dental health through routine dental cleanings, brushing your dog's teeth, and giving him dental-friendly chews, you can prevent severe periodontal disease and its consequences.

Ear and eye care

Ear and eye care are relatively easy and simple. I tend to leave Marty McFly's ears and eyes alone unless there is a problem. Lucky for us, we haven't had any issues. The only time I really clean out his ears is after he has gone swimming or has been given a bath because water in the ear canal can cause irritation and potentially lead to ear infections. If your dog is scratching his ears a lot and/or there is a yeast-like smell, he may have an infection. It is best to deal with this as soon as possible because, left untreated, an ear infection can cause major damage.

Photo Courtesy of Sally Herron

The best way to clean a dog's ears is to use a veterinarian-approved ear cleaning solution and fill your dog's ear canal. Once you can see the liquid, gently massage the ear at its base for about 30 seconds. During this, you will hear a squishing sound; that is the solution dislodging and breaking up debris and buildup. After you finish massaging his ear, your dog will shake his head. Use a cotton swab and gently clean out any leftover liquid and debris.

Repeat these steps on the opposite side. Make sure not to touch the applicator tip to the ear itself, as it can introduce bacteria into the ear. If this is challenging, wipe the tip of the applicator with alcohol prior to use, between ears, and after use.

I have generally left Marty McFly's eyes alone unless there was an issue. He has never had excessive tears like some small dogs do. I will sometimes wipe away his eye goobers, but other than that, I leave well enough alone. Your veterinarian will check your dog's eyes and ears during your dog's annual checkup, just to confirm everything is in working order.

Anal glands

Many people don't realize that dogs have anal glands, which are two scent sacs that are located just inside the rectum. These are usually expressed when a dog defecates, and it leaves a small oily coating on the feces. This is another way in which dogs mark their territory, and it acts almost like their personal signature. In the wild, this would let other wolves know who was in the area, whether it was an alpha male, a breeding female, or what have you.

However, sometimes dogs have issues with their anal glands, which can lead to them excessively rubbing their butt on the carpet, licking back there, or even having the glands rupture. If your dog starts showing these behaviors or looks like he has ruptured his anal glands, which will look very red and inflamed with potentially a small hole visible, you should schedule an appointment to get him seen by your veterinarian. Some dogs go their whole lives without ever having an issue, while others have to go to the vet routinely to have their anal glands manually expressed.

CHAPTER SEVENTEEN
Basic Health Care

Routine vet visits

Visiting the veterinarian routinely is essential for maintaining your dog's health. Routine visits allow the veterinarian to do a full physical exam on your pet to assess any changes over the last six months to a year, conduct a dental assessment, update preventative measures like vaccines and flea and tick prevention, as well as run any routine blood work.

When your dog is young, he will need to go to the vet more often in order to get a puppy series of vaccines and deworming. Once he is over a year old, he will more than likely only have to go to the vet annually for a yearly wellness visit, barring any sick pet exams. Once your dog starts to get older, your veterinarian may recommend exams every six months and/or blood work every six months to monitor his health more closely.

Currently, Marty McFly goes to the vet every six months for blood-work to monitor his kidney disease that has started to develop, along with chronic hypoparathyroidism. This is important because he is on long-term medications, and we need to monitor his levels more frequently than the average dog.

Flea and tick prevention

Fleas

Fleas are small insects that survive by feeding on blood from animals and humans. Their bites can cause discomfort, itchiness, and irritation. Many dogs are allergic to flea bites and can have more severe symptoms, such as flaky skin, scabs, hot spots, and hair loss. If your dog gets fleas, he can transmit them to you and eventually infest your home. Once your home has an infestation, it becomes very hard to get rid of them.

Photo Courtesy
of Rebecca & Gabe Morales

HEALTH WATCH

Identifying Primary Lens Luxation

Jack Russell Terriers can be prone to developing primary lens luxation, an inherited condition that causes weakness in the connective ligaments, which hold the lens in place. This disorder usually presents itself in adulthood and can lead to an increase in ocular pressure and inflammation. Any change in the appearance of your dog's eyes, including redness or cloudiness, could indicate a problem. Squinting, lethargy, and increased tears are also signs of this disease. Untreated lens luxation can cause blindness, so don't hesitate to consult your veterinarian if you suspect this issue.

Fleas have four life cycle stages—egg, larva, pupa, and adult. The adult fleas are the ones that you can see living on your dog, and they will leave behind dirt-looking specks, which are digested blood and eggs that they have laid. These eggs will hatch in 1-10 days and will drop wherever your dog has been. Once they hatch into larvae, they begin to move across their host and start feeding on the digested blood from the adult fleas. This digested blood is also commonly known as flea dirt.

During the pupa stage, fleas will form cocoons in areas of your home such as the sofa, carpet, or bed until a warm-bodied host appears. Fleas can wait in these cocoons for several days up to an entire year. Once they hatch, they become full-bodied adults, ready to infest and reproduce on other animals.

If your dog is itching a lot, you notice redness, or if you happen to notice flea dirt, I recommend you bring your dog to the veterinarian. They can give your dog a medicated bath that will kill the adult fleas. They may send you home with medicated shampoo just to make sure any larvae or eggs are also eliminated from your dog's fur and skin. Wash all the dog beds, bedding, and soft toys in hot soapy water. Repeat frequently until the infestation is eliminated.

Wash your own bedding, throw rugs, bathmats, blankets, cushions, and any other soft fabric material in hot soapy water.

Vacuum all carpet and floors, as well as curtains and upholstered furniture. You will need to vacuum on a regular basis until the infestation is gone. If you have a vacuum with bags, the bags need to be thrown away in an outside bin immediately. If you have a canister vacuum, empty the contents into a bag, close securely, throw away in an outside bin, and clean the vacuum canister.

Apply a nontoxic flea treatment to your yard, and make sure to keep your grass short and any brush trimmed. Make sure your yard is protected from wildlife as best you can because raccoons, rabbits, and other wildlife can also carry fleas.

Make sure to vacuum out your car if your dog has ridden in it since he was infested.

Start your dog on a monthly preventative to protect him in the future.

Ticks

Ticks are another insect that can affect your dog's health and well-being. Ticks attach to your dog by inserting their mouth into your dog's skin, and some ticks even have a sticky substance they secrete to essentially glue themselves to the skin. After they have attached, they will begin feeding on your dog's blood. Ticks are most commonly found after they have been engorged for some time and become filled and swollen with your dog's blood. At their attachment site, there is usually some redness and irritation. Once the tick has gotten its fill, it may fall off your dog.

Ticks are a vector for diseases that can not only transmit to your dog, but he can also transmit these diseases to you. Lyme disease is a serious illness in dogs caused by a bacterium Borrelia burgdorferi that is transmit-

ted from the tick's saliva to a dog's (or human's) bloodstream. If a dog gets Lyme disease, he may have to be hospitalized; he will have to be on antibiotics for at least 30 days. This disease may lead to severe kidney, cardiac, and/or neurological deficits. It is better to prevent Lyme disease than to treat it.

It can be very challenging to prevent your dog's exposure to ticks because ticks are hard to see and can get on your dog during any type of outdoor activity. The best way to prevent ticks is to get your dog on routine tick control products and check your dog for ticks daily if you are in a high-risk tick area, after

Photo Courtesy of Angeline Smit

hiking, and especially if your dog is doing any type of hunting or fieldwork. If you find a tick on your dog, it is important to remove it right away and look for any other ticks.

Ticks like warm places to hide and attach on your dog. The most common areas ticks will attach are in and around the ears, around the eyelids, under the collar, under the front legs, between the toes, between the back legs, and around the tail. Once you find the tick, the best way to remove it is by using a pair of clean fine-tipped tweezers. Try to grasp the parasite as close to the skin as possible. Pull upward with steady, even pressure. Make sure not to twist, crush, or jerk the tick out because you can leave part of the mouth attached, which can cause an infection. After removing the tick, thoroughly clean the bite area with soap and water or rubbing alcohol. Dispose of the tick by placing it in alcohol, placing it in a sealed bag or container, wrapping it tightly in tape, or flushing it down the toilet.

There are a variety of different types of flea and tick prevention products on the market currently. There are some that only cover flea and ticks, and there are some products that will also prevent intestinal parasites and heartworms. Here are some of the varying flea and tick prevention options currently available:

- Flea and tick collar: Usually around $60, this is a plastic collar that you place around your dog's neck alongside their other collar. It will protect them from fleas and ticks of all life stages up to eight months. A lot of people like this option, but I have had a young dog actually chew the collar off their housemate and eat part of the collar, which led to an emergency visit to the veterinarian.

- Capstar is a one-time flea treatment that is usually given when your dog already has fleas. It is an oral product that starts working in 30 minutes. It costs about $40 and is more of a treatment instead of a prevention method.

- Topical flea and tick prevention is a monthly treatment that costs about $70 for a six-month supply. It contains small applicators which you will crack open and apply directly to the skin between your dog's shoulder blades.

Some topical flea and tick prevention also prevent heartworms, mange, and intestinal parasites and is about $120 for a six-month supply. This is a great combination prevention product, so you only have to remember one thing to give monthly instead of multiple.

There are also monthly oral tablets that are combination prevention products that prevent heartworm, fleas, ticks, and intestinal parasites. Their cost is about $130 for a six-month supply and may be a good option for treat-driven dogs.

If you are unsure which product would be best for your dog feel free to ask your veterinarian. Most of these products are by prescription anyway. This conversation will be a part of your annual health exam with your veterinarian. Also, if you are using a combination prevention product, you may need to get a heartworm test before starting.

Parasite prevention

Heartworms

Heartworms are a parasite transmitted by a mosquito into a dog through a mosquito bite, and as they mature, these parasites, or worms, can grow up to a foot long and live in your dog's heart, lungs, and blood vessels. If left untreated, they can cause severe lung disease, heart failure, and significant organ damage. Heartworms tend to be more common in the southern part of the United States, but with the increased transportation of dogs around the country, the disease has an opportunity to be wider spread.

In a dog that has been infected by heartworms, the adult heartworms will release their offspring, called microfilariae, into the bloodstream. When a mosquito bites the dog, it not only gets blood, but it also gets these microfilariae, which then become infective larvae within the mosquito. When the mosquito with the infective larvae bites another dog, it spreads this larva to that dog through the bite wound. It takes the larvae about six to seven months to develop into adult heartworms. Then the adult heartworms mate and release their offspring into the bloodstream, starting the cycle all over again. Inside a dog, the heartworm's lifespan is five to seven years, and the worms can reach from four to 12 inches in length.

Veterinarians can do a blood test to see if your dog has heartworms. Most rescues will do this on their incoming dogs, especially if they are coming from the southern part of the United States. This antigen test detects specific proteins, called antigens, which are released by the adult female heartworm. They can detect these antigens even if there is only one adult heartworm in the dog. The earliest these antigens can be found is five months after the dog has been bitten by an infected mosquito. There is a second test that tests for microfilariae in a dog's bloodstream, usually six months post-mosquito bite.

Dogs that are seven months of age and older should be tested for heartworm prior to starting prevention. Some dogs may not present with any symptoms unless they have a large infestation of heartworms. If a dog who has heartworm is not tested and is just started on prevention, he will remain infested with the adult heartworms until he starts to show symptoms and becomes sick. In addition, giving a dog heartworm prevention when he already has heartworms can be very harmful or even deadly. Dogs with a lower worm burden may have an occasional cough and tiredness after moderate activity. Those with a higher worm burden will have a sicklier appearance, a persistent cough, tiredness after mild activity, trouble breathing, and issues with blood circulation.

There is a treatment for heartworm disease, but it is long, costly, and is not easy on the dog. The treatment itself can be dangerous because it may be toxic to the dog's body and can cause serious complications, such as blood clots to the lungs. Treatment is expensive because it requires multiple visits with your veterinarian, X-rays, bloodwork, injections, and hospitalizations.

The best treatment is prevention. Heartworm disease is easy to prevent with a monthly chewable tablet that is available by prescription from your veterinarian. Even if your dog is on prevention, annual heartworm testing is recommended. In addition, a lot of heartworm prevention medication also prevents intestinal parasites like whipworm, tapeworm, roundworm, and hookworm.

Whipworms

Whipworms are intestinal parasites that are about a quarter of an inch in length and live inside the cecum, the first part of the large intestine, and the length of the large intestine. They cause severe irritation in the lining of those organs, which leads to watery, bloody diarrhea, weight loss, and general debilitation in dogs, but especially young or immune-compromised dogs. Whipworms cause the most disease compared to any other intestinal parasite.

Whipworms lay microscopic eggs in the stool and will be able to reinfect another dog in 10–60 days. These eggs can survive in the environment for up to five years. The mature eggs are then ingested by another dog and will hatch within the intestinal tract and become mature adults in the lower intestinal tract, completing their life cycle.

Whipworms are usually diagnosed after a dog presents with bloody diarrhea and the veterinarian does a fecal test. A fecal test is a sample of the dog's stool, which is examined under a microscope. Usually, this test must be repeated a couple of times because whipworms do not pass eggs on a regular basis, and the female whipworm does not lay eggs until 11–12 weeks after she herself has hatched. Because of this, it is common practice to treat dogs with diarrhea with a whipworm dewormer even if they were not detected upon fecal examination. All treatments for whipworm are given in two doses, three to four weeks apart. Since whipworm eggs are so hardy, it is possible for dogs to get reinfected easily, so it is advisable to use a preventative medication that is usually included in a heartworm prevention treatment.

Photo Courtesy of Venus Gualandri

Tapeworms

Tapeworms are flat, segmented intestinal parasites that have hook-like mouthparts that they use to attach to the walls of the small intestines. The adult worms may reach up to 11 inches in length and will detach segments, which are passed through the feces of an infected dog. Usually, these segments look like grains of rice. Sometimes owners will notice these little segments moving in the hairs around the anus or on the surface of freshly passed feces. If left alone, these segments will die and eventually break open to release a fertilized egg into the environment. Each segment can contain up to 20 tapeworm eggs. Tapeworms have to first pass through an intermediate host before they can infect a dog, and usually, that host is a flea.

When the eggs are released to the environment, flea larvae feast on the eggs, and the eggs then develop within the flea as the flea matures. When a flea infests a dog, the dog will chew on his skin and inadvertently ingest these infected fleas that are carrying the tapeworms. As the flea becomes ingested, the tapeworm egg is released, hatches, and then takes hold within the intestinal lining. Tapeworms don't usually cause serious health problems in adult dogs, though they definitely irritate them, but in puppies, tapeworm infestations can cause intestinal blockages and anemia.

More often than not, diagnosis is made by the observation of the segments found in the feces or around the anus, and treatment is relatively easy. Your veterinarian will use a parasiticide that causes the parasite to be digested like normal food within the intestines. It is very important to protect your dogs from fleas because that will inherently prevent them from tapeworms. This is also important because you yourself can get tapeworms from your dog, depending on the type of tapeworm he is infected with.

Roundworms

Roundworms are parasites that are also known as nematodes or ascarids that live freely within the intestine and thrive off the partially digested intestinal contents. There are two species of concern, which are Toxocara canis and Toxicaris leonine. Toxocara canis causes more significant disease in dogs and can also be transmitted to humans. Roundworms are the most common gastrointestinal worm found in dogs.

Infected dogs will shed the microscopic roundworm eggs in their feces, and other dogs will sniff or lick those infected feces and become infected themselves. Roundworm eggs can also be transmitted by other animals, such as rodents, earthworms, cockroaches, and birds. If a dog eats any of these creatures, it can also become infected with the parasite. Once the egg is in the dog's system, it goes through a complicated life cycle before the roundworms mature enough to be found within the intestinal tract. It is important to make sure breeding females have roundworm prevention because the roundworm larvae can actually cross the placenta and infect the unborn puppy, or the larvae can transfer into the mother's mammary glands and be transmitted to the puppy that way.

Roundworms most commonly affect puppies and can reduce their development and growth by robbing the puppy of the vital nutrition it needs to grow. Roundworms complete their life cycles in immature dogs. As puppies grow, the larval stages of the roundworm become arrested and are enclosed in a cyst within the puppy's muscle. They can remain in these cysts for months to years.

Usually, roundworm is diagnosed when puppies present with stunted growth, potbelly, and recurrent diarrhea. The veterinarian will take a fecal sample and look at it under a microscope to detect any eggs. The treatment is simple and effective, and roundworms can actually be prevented by using a monthly preventative tablet or chewable.

Hookworms

Hookworms are another form of intestinal parasite that attach themselves to the lining of the intestinal walls. They get their name from the hook-like mouthparts and are only about one-eighth of an inch long, making them difficult to see with the naked eye. Despite their small size, they can ingest a large amount of blood, and a large infestation can cause inflammation within the intestines and can even make your dog anemic.

Hookworms are most commonly found in warm, moist environments where there is a lot of overcrowding. They can be a common problem in animal shelters because of the constant spraying down of kennels.

Hookworms can infect your dog through oral transmission, through the skin, through the mother's placenta before birth, or through the mother's milk. The female hookworms can pass hundreds of microscopic eggs in the feces of the infected dog. Larvae then hatch and can remain infective within the soil for weeks or months. Another dog can then inadvertently swallow hookworm larvae, where it will move to the intestinal tract to finish its life cycle. If a dog lies on contaminated ground, hookworm larvae can burrow through the skin and make their way to the lungs and trachea, where the dog may cough up and swallow the larvae, leading them to the intestinal tract.

Most commonly, infected dogs will have diarrhea and also show weakness, pale gums, and poor blood circulation because the hookworms inject an anticoagulant into the bloodstream to prevent the blood from clotting. This will cause the intestine to continue bleeding after the hookworm has detached from the intestinal wall. Some dogs will present with severe weight loss, bloody diarrhea, a dull and dry coat, or failure to grow properly. Puppies can die from severe hookworm infections. The diagnosis is the same as other intestinal parasites, which includes a fecal exam done by your veterinarian.

There are several drugs that can treat a hookworm infestation, and most of them are given orally. This treatment is often given twice, the second dose being two to four weeks after the first. If your dog does become infected with hookworms, it is important to make sure you pick up his feces right away

Photo Courtesy
of Krystal Latour

and dispose of them properly. Use gloves to place the feces in plastic bags and place them in your trash can. Your dog's monthly heartworm preventative should also take care of hookworms.

Intestinal parasites can have severe consequences in puppies, including anemia and developmental stunting. Healthy adult animals have less serious issues with intestinal parasites, but they can lead to discomfort, gastroenteritis, vomiting, and difficulty defecating. Some intestinal parasites are zoonotic, meaning they can be transferred to humans. Because we have such close relationships with our dogs, it is wise to give them preventative medication for intestinal parasites not only for their benefit but for yours as well.

Currently, most heartworm preventative medications also prevent the majority of these most common intestinal parasites. Your veterinarian may want to run a heartworm test and fecal test before starting these monthly preventative medications, but once your dog is on them and you are consistent with them, you can prevent a lot of unwanted discomfort in your dog and save your wallet.

Microchipping

I am a big fan of microchipping dogs because it provides a secure, reliable, and permanent form of identification for your pet. All veterinary clinics, rescues, and humane societies usually have a microchip scanner, so if your dog gets lost, someone can bring him to any of these types of locations, get him scanned, and get him back home to you ASAP.

Microchipping does hurt—it is a big needle—but after a minute or two, your dog will forget it ever happened. If you have a dog that is going in for a procedure that requires anesthesia, like getting spayed or neutered for puppies, I recommend having the animal microchipped at the same time. This allows your dog to be under anesthesia and not be aware of the needle at all. If you are rescuing your Jack Russell, you should ask the rescue organization if the dog has been microchipped and what steps you can take to get the information transferred to your name. Some rescues will keep it under their name, so the dogs are always returned to them, but this is not always the case.

Many people keep collars and tags on their dogs as a form of identification, but I have had tags fall off, collars get caught and trapped on something, or heard of dogs sneaking out the backyard or bolting out the front door unexpectedly. I want to make sure that no matter what the scenario is, my Marty McFly will be able to find his way back home.

Supplements

I will always recommend you speak to your veterinarian before starting any supplements. This is especially important in older dogs who may be on long-term medications or have chronic illnesses. Your veterinarian will know what supplements are appropriate for your dog, what amount you should be giving him, and what negative interactions may occur if multiple supplements or medications are given at the same time.

Fish oil is a popular supplement in dogs because of the myriad benefits it can provide—everything from a shinier coat to joint mobility. This is one of the few supplements that I stand strongly behind because it can help dogs across the span of their lifetime and has multiple benefits. Fish oil can help promote a silky coat and can help with heart health, relieving allergies, and alleviating joint pain. This is due to the omega-3 fatty acids that are rich in this supplement. Dosing and type are important considerations to take note of, so good research and a conversation with your veterinarian will put you on the right path to finding what is appropriate for your Jack Russell.

In addition to fish oil, I find that glucosamine and chondroitin, usually in combination, work wonders for older dogs, dogs with joint and mobility issues, and in some cases, post-orthopedic trauma or surgery. Many veterinarians will recommend this supplement for geriatric dogs with arthritis, and I have personally seen a lot of dogs flourish with this supplement. However, I always recommend that owners discuss this with their veterinarian because the human version of this supplement may vary greatly from the dog version, and it is good to make sure that all of the ingredients are safe for your dog.

Vaccines

Having your dog fully vaccinated is one of the most important parts of being a dog owner. Vaccines prevent dogs from getting infectious diseases.

The Bordetella vaccine prevents the highly infectious bacterium Bordetella bronchiseptica, which causes severe fits of coughing, vomiting, and in some rare cases, seizures and death. This bacterium is the main cause of kennel cough and is often required for every dog going to doggy daycare or staying overnight at a kennel.

Canine distemper is a highly contagious virus that affects the respiratory, gastrointestinal, and nervous systems in dogs. It is spread through airborne exposure from an infected animal to another. It can even be transmitted through shared food or water bowls. There is no cure for distemper, and puppies who contract distemper and survive often live with long-term disabilities and deficits. However, most dogs or puppies who contract distemper do not live. This is why getting the puppy series for distemper is so important.

Canine hepatitis is another highly contagious viral infection that attacks the liver, kidneys, spleen, lungs, and eyes of the affected dog. This virus is unrelated to the human form of hepatitis. There is no cure for this disease, but veterinarians can treat the symptoms, and many dogs can overcome the disease. This disease can be prevented by getting your dog vaccinated with the DHPP vaccine series.

Canine parainfluenza is another virus that can cause kennel cough. It is not a severe disease but is usually highly transmissible, so many kennels and doggy daycare centers require the vaccine.

Parvovirus is a very contagious virus that can affect all dogs but especially those that are unvaccinated. It attacks the gastrointestinal system, causing your dog to lose his appetite, vomit, start a fever, and produce severe bloody diarrhea. There is no cure, and often veterinarians have to prevent dehydration from occurring. Many puppies die from parvo, and those that live usually undergo long-term hospitalization on intravenous fluids to survive.

Rabies is another zoonotic disease that can be transmitted to humans from a dog's saliva to a human's bloodstream through a bite. Your dog is required by law to have the rabies vaccine.

At the age of six to eight weeks, your puppy should get vaccines to prevent distemper and parvoviruses. Usually, this is a combination vaccine known as the DHPP vaccine. The DHPP vaccine prevents distemper, adenovirus (hepatitis), parainfluenza, and parvovirus. Your puppy will receive this vaccine in a series every four to six weeks until he is four months old. Every one to two years, he will need to get the DHPP vaccine, and every one to three years, he will need to get a rabies vaccine. There are other vaccines your veterinarian may recommend based on your dog's individual lifestyle.

CHAPTER EIGHTEEN

Long-term Health Care

> "
>
> *Jack Russells regularly live to be 15 years or older. They may lose their sight and/or hearing, but they will still be eager to please, able to sniff out a treat or toy, and will still want to cuddle. It is important to work with your vet to keep your senior dog free from pain should he have joint problems. Your older dog may suffer from dementia or incontinence. Both of these conditions can be managed to keep the dog comfortable and your home safe and clean. Always, always look for solutions to help make your senior Jack Russell comfortable. Dogs give us so much love—it is our responsibility to help them age well.*
>
> PATTI STORMS
> *Rabble Rouser Jack Russell Terriers*
>
> "

What age is considered a "senior dog" in JRT's

Jack Russell Terriers can begin to be considered seniors between the ages of eight and 10 years. There is no single change that indicates this transition, but there are a series of small changes. One of the most common changes in aging dogs that people tend to notice is the color of their dogs' eyes and how their hearing tends to worsen. If you notice sudden changes, seek out your veterinarian immediately because this may be due to some inflammation or infection, but if it is just due to aging, your dog may never be able to regain what was lost. Dogs tend to develop "gray" eyes, which is a normal changing of the lens that does not affect vision. Cataracts, on

the other hand, can cause significant vision loss and may need to be
addressed surgically.

Photo Courtesy
of Demi Elliot

Eyes becoming cloudy or difficulty seeing is usually an indication
of aging. Cloudiness in the eyes is
called nuclear sclerosis and usually
happens gradually. It doesn't necessarily affect vision, but it can be
a sign of cataracts or another eye
disease. Your dog may have issues
catching his toys, may bump into
things, or have trouble finding treats
dropped on the floor, which can all
be indications of vision issues. A
consultation with your veterinarian
and a veterinary ophthalmologist
can help address these issues.

Hearing loss is due to the damage or death of the tiny hairs inside your
dog's ear. Hearing changes are common in aging dogs, and it can be hard
to decipher what is selective hearing and what is actually hearing difficulty.
Selective hearing is a term many dog owners associate with dogs who seem
to choose when they want to listen or not. For example, you are at the park,
and you call your dog's name, but he decides to finish what he is sniffing
before he comes to you. This can be challenging when trying to decipher if
your dog is going deaf.

If you are concerned about your dog going deaf, definitely talk to your
veterinarian, but you can also do a small assessment at home. When your
dog is sleeping, call his name and see if he responds, or if he is lying down,
drop something on one side of him, or clap your hands and see if he reacts.
Do it again on the other side after the dog is relaxed again. If your dog is
exhibiting signs of deafness, you may want to change the way you interact
with him. Perhaps using more hand signals or alerting him to go outside by
showing him his leash can help make communication easier.

Slowing down, less energy, or trouble getting around can also be signs
of aging in your dog. This may present as a hesitation in jumping into the
car, getting on the couch, or climbing stairs and may progress even further to weakness in the back legs and difficulty getting up. These can be
signs of arthritis, joint inflammation, or other degenerative disease associated with aging and can be managed early on with veterinarian-guided

supplementation, but also by shortening your dog's walks, using ramps for him to get on the couch or bed, and perhaps getting him an orthopedic bed to sleep on.

A change in weight can also indicate your dog is transitioning into the senior phase. Usually, senior dogs tend to gain weight because they are not burning as many calories. Your veterinarian may recommend switching your dog to a senior diet, which is formulated for aging pets. If your dog loses weight rapidly, this may be indicative of severe disease and should be brought to your veterinarian's attention immediately. Because senior dogs are less active, you may also notice a decrease in muscle mass, which tends to be common in older dogs. If you have any concerns, speak to your veterinarian.

Some senior dogs will develop incontinence or have difficulty going to the bathroom. Incontinence is a lack of control over the bladder or the sphincter muscle of the rectum. There are degrees of incontinence, and it usually presents small, perhaps as a small wet spot on a dog's bedding that you notice after he gets up. It can progress to loss of full bladder function that may present as your dog urinating on the way out the door to go potty. This can be caused by aging or some underlying health condition; your veterinarian will be able to help you figure out what is going on.

If it is incontinence, there are medications that can help prevent this from happening. Stool incontinence can be a bit more difficult and may indicate neurological changes. Some potty changes may be small, like a dog having to take multiple steps when defecating because squatting to defecate puts stress on his arthritic joints. Supplements like chondroitin and glucosamine can help the joints, and a probiotic can help the stools become softer so they pass a little bit easier.

There can also be mental and cognitive changes that may occur in your dog that resemble what we know as dementia in humans. In dogs, we call this canine cognitive dysfunction syndrome or CCDS. CCDS can change your dog's day-to-day behavior, and he may begin to start fearing familiar people or objects, have changes to sleeping behaviors, have increased barking or vocalization, forget commands he once knew, have confusion,

FUN FACT
Oldest Jack Russell Terrier

According to Guinness World Records, the oldest Jack Russell Terrier lived to be 20 years old. His name was Willie, and he passed away in 2014. Jack Russell Terriers typically live an average of 13 to 16 years.

Photo Courtesy of TJ Carter

go to the bathroom in the house, and have changes to activity levels. Unfortunately, there is no cure for CCDS, but your veterinarian can help discuss options with you.

Your veterinarian is going to be your primary source of help and guidance in helping your dog transition into the senior phase. They can help determine if there are any underlying medical conditions that might be affecting your dog's health and can also prescribe any treatments or recommendations for supplementation. Try to stay in tune with your dog and see how he is doing with the adjustments you have made.

Some things will take time. Acupuncture for arthritis may seem like it isn't making any improvements after the first or second appointment, but after some time, it can start making a significant difference. A holistic approach coupled with your veterinarian recommendations can give you a well-rounded care plan to help your dog age gracefully for many years.

As our dogs get older, some of our routines and behaviors will need to be adapted based on their needs. It is important to remember that age is not a disease and that we just might need to make some modifications in order to help our dogs age gracefully.

Some important steps in taking care of a senior dog include:

- Feeding an age-appropriate diet
- Getting regular exercise
- Committing to routine check-ups with your veterinarian
- Maintaining oral health through toothbrushing, dental chews, and dental cleaning at the vet
- Staying consistent with preventative health care such as vaccines and protection from intestinal parasites
- Regular grooming, including nail trimming
- Providing special accommodations such as ramps or more rugs on slippery floors
- And, of course, spending quality time with your dog.

Old age in Jack Russells is beyond 10 and much more. Many Jacks see 15–17 years. Sometimes, though, seniors forget to slow down, and it is up to people to be sure their canines take it easier. DNA testing is now available to breeders so they can eliminate many of the serious issues that may arise in old age. Terrier eyes often show the first signs of aging. Senior cataracts can be seen in older dogs and can be removed surgically. A condition called nuclear sclerosis is more common as dogs age; it is a clouding of the lens. It does not affect vision until long into old age, but can inhibit depth perception. There is no cure or treatment, but it rarely affects the quality of a dog's life. It appears as a bluish tint in the eye. Jacks start to slow down with time, appreciate a spot of sun to nap in, and like a moderate walk around the block or through a field. If they have a good diet and are offered chews during their lifetime, their teeth can hold up very well. Mentally, Jack Russells normally stay alert and appreciate games and activity well into their senior years.

SUE ANNE WILSON
West Elk Terriers

As Marty McFly has started to get older, I have made some modifications to our normal routines. When getting in the car or up into my bed, I no longer encourage him to jump up; instead, I pick him up. I have gotten him a heated orthopedic bed to make him more comfortable when he sleeps. Instead of having him run beside my bike on the boardwalk, I got him a dog cart that attaches to the back of my bike so he can still enjoy the ride but does not have to run on the hard pavement. I make sure to exercise him on forgiving surfaces like sand and grass in order to be gentler on his joints and bones. Some of these needs for modification happened after I noted a change in behavior, such as Marty McFly hesitating before jumping in the car.

Helping your JRT age gracefully

66

Unfortunately, age affects everyone and everything. The average life span is 15 years for a Jack Russell Terrier. So, one moment, you are dealing with an unruly bundle of energy, and the next, your best friend is moving a lot slower and is a little arthritic and sleeping a lot more. Your senior best friend can't hear and see you as well, but what will never change is his love for you. Just like when your dog was a puppy, patience, love, and common sense will go a long way.

COLLEEN REEDER
Snowcrest Jack Russell Terriers

99

Getting a baseline health profile of your dog midway through his life allows you and your veterinarian to monitor any changes as your dog ages. These baseline health profiles are essentially what your annual exams are about, but should include blood work, forethought in nutritional support both in diet and supplementation, and follow-through with annual blood-work to detect changes early on.

A body map is another tool many veterinarians use for dogs that are starting to develop lumps and bumps. This body map is essentially a two-dimensional drawing of your dog and indicates locations of these lumps and bumps, their characteristics, and the results from fine needle aspirations, whether they were cancerous or benign. Marty McFly has had his body map for about three years now because he has had benign lipomas (fatty tumors) that we have been watching, as well as a tiny mass on his liver that we picked up during an ultrasound. Due to this mass on his liver, we also do a health screening ultrasound yearly to assess any changes. This is an expensive diagnostic, but one that I have budgeted for annually in order to help him continue to age gracefully.

Maintaining good nutrition and mobility can be challenging, especially as your dog's activity levels change. If you notice your dog is becoming less active as he ages, you will want to pay attention to his weight. It will be a lot easier for him to put on the pounds, and even just one pound on a Jack Russell can make a significant difference to overall health.

In combination with treatments, supplements, and diets recommended by your veterinarian, you can also discuss what type of holistic or alternative medicine options would be beneficial to your dog. There is an expanding animal holistic scene that is thriving. Some of the treatments are visibly beneficial, and some may be more mentally or spiritually releasing to the owner. Here are some of the treatments that have been shown to create positive change and support for aging dogs.

- **Acupuncture** can help with a range of health elements in the senior dog, especially those with inflammatory ailments, diseases affecting the spine, elbow and hip dysplasia, arthritis, and in some situations, it can help with gastrointestinal issues.

- **Hydrotherapy** can involve a few different methods. Some can be as simple as warm baths to relieve muscle and joint pain, and some include walking on a treadmill where the dog is submerged just enough to become buoyant, which can help with mobility in arthritic dogs. Swimming is another hydrotherapy method that is used often in the recovery of injury but can also help manage chronic pain.

- **Massage** is just as you would imagine for a human but with your dog. Massage focuses on rubbing muscles to reduce pain. It can help with arthritis and other musculoskeletal chronic conditions.

- **Chiropractic** work is relatively new to the field of veterinary medicine and may be able to help your dog if they have spinal issues. However, use caution and speak to your veterinarian first, especially if your dog has any disc disease or spinal conditions, as this may actually complicate them further. If you think chiropractic therapy might help your dog, consult your veterinarian, request recommendations, and look to see if the individual or facility is accredited or supported by veterinarians or the veterinary board.

Assessing your dog's quality of life

Assessing your dog's quality of life is something that you cannot do alone. Your veterinarian is going to be you and your dog's best advocate and resource. Your veterinarian will never tell you what you should do, but they will help give you all your options, and once those options are exhausted, they will let you know. A good veterinarian will go as far as you want to in order to help your dog as long as it is for the continued benefit of your dog.

I have told many clients to get two jars, one for good days and one for bad days. When your dog has a good day, put a stone or coin in the good day jar, and vice versa for the bad day jar. Once the bad day jar gets higher than the good day jar, you may want to really assess your dog's quality of life. Keeping a journal can also help you catalog your dog's changes and look at averages over the week. Whatever works best for you. But it is important to remember that age is not a disease. Just because your dog may have some blindness, deafness, or some urinary incontinence does not mean he no longer has a good quality of life.

Some things to look for are whether your dog is still enjoying those small moments, playing with his favorite toy, getting a tasty snack, wagging his tail, and getting excited to get up and go outside. Here are some questions to ask yourself when considering your dog's quality of life:

1.   Is he feeling pain? Is his pain no longer manageable with treatment and medications?

2.   Has he completely lost the ability to urinate or defecate normally?

3.   Has he started experiencing seizures?

4.   Has he become violent or unsafe to others?

5.   How is he eating? Is his appetite severely decreased or nonexistent?

6.   Is your dog no longer acting normally?

7.   Has your dog's chronic condition become worse with time?

8.   Are you financially able to continue treatment?

9.   Is your veterinary team supportive of euthanasia?

Some veterinarians may have a survey form you can use that asks a series of questions on a scale and, depending on your score, may help guide you on your dog's quality of life. If this is of interest to you, and your veterinarian doesn't have it, you can do an internet search for Assessing Quality of

Life for your Companion Animal and Making End of Life Decisions; you may find a survey that can help you.

Unfortunately, this process is not black or white, and there are a lot of moments in a dog's aging and decline where it may be most humane to euthanize him. It is dependent on how the dog takes treatment, what you can afford, and what is available to you. Not everyone has a veterinary school right up the road and a bank account set aside for a dog's care, and that's okay. It is important to draw that line of what's best for your dog and make your decision with confidence, support, and as much consideration as possible.

The rainbow bridge

One of the hardest decisions you will ever have to make with your dog is when it is time to say goodbye. Sometimes, dogs make this decision for us by dying at home of their own accord, but often we are the ones who have to make the choice. After 10 years of working in veterinary medicine, I still cry during euthanasia appointments, but I find that there is a small blessing in them. Our dogs give us so much in their too-short lifetimes. They teach us to love, to be patient, and to be kind, all while they go about their days loving us unconditionally as if it is as easy as breathing. I look at euthanasia as the one gift we can give dogs, the gift of allowing them to let go and to die peacefully.

I have been through a lot of euthanasia experiences, some as good as you could hope for and some that are heart-wrenchingly terrible. I know this subject is hard to talk about, and I understand if you want to skip this, but I believe it is important to not only understand the process but also understand what is going on within the veterinary side of it. That way, when the day comes, many years from now, you will be prepared.

First of all, be open and honest with your veterinarian about what is going on. It is rare that a vet will straight out tell you to euthanize, but the vet will also give you the support and guidance you will need to make your decision. I had a dog that had multiple neurological issues going on, tons of diagnostics, medications all day long, and he never got better. I toiled for months making the decision, and I had the whole veterinary team supporting me with every choice I made. I don't think I could have done it without them.

Once you have made the decision and set the appointment, try to spend those last days or hours spoiling your dog rotten. Steak? You betcha! Maple bacon logs? How about three? Also, know that you may have options to choose as to where you want euthanasia to happen. Some veterinarians come to a client's house and euthanize an animal in the comfort of its home rather than having a pet come to the veterinary clinic. If this is something you would prefer, make sure to ask about it. There may be a higher cost, but you and your dog's comfort are the most important thing.

Try to be present. Your dog has been there for all the good and the bad events in your life; be there for him. I know it is hard; nobody wants to see the passing of their pet, but in my experience, there is nothing harder than taking a pet from an owner and having to let him go in the hands of strangers. So, if you can be there, please do it for your dog. Your warmth, scent, and love are the last thing your dog should experience before he goes.

The process may vary from veterinarian to veterinarian, but it is usually very similar. You will need to fill out paperwork with the receptionist or the veterinary staff and pay for the procedure. This is usually done prior to the euthanasia, so you can feel free to leave when it is completed.

After all the paperwork is done, the decisions are made on what to do with the body, cremation, clay paw memento, and so on, a technician will come to set an intravenous catheter. Sometimes, they will take your dog to the back; sometimes, they will do this in the room. I personally always try to do it in the room, but sometimes if the veins are tough to hit or the dog is very sick, doing it in the back is easier and quicker because there is more staff available, better lighting, and your dog may be calmer without you present.

The intravenous catheter allows your dog to be poked only once and helps maintain access to the cardiovascular system to make the process as quick and smooth as possible.

While you are saying your last goodbyes, there are some things I have always loved to do. If the dog is still eating and has an appetite, I love to give him the things he couldn't have before, such as a chocolate donut or cat food. I've given dogs a $20 steak before they go. I feel it helps distract both you and your dog from what's going on and may even put a little smile on your face when you see the dog's eyes light up after the first time he has ever had chocolate. Once you are ready for the veterinarian to come in, you can alert the veterinary staff; some may have a call bell you can press, and the veterinarian will be alerted.

Once the veterinarian comes in, they will talk to you about the procedure if the veterinary staff hasn't already. Feel free to ask questions. The process doesn't hurt, and it usually goes very smoothly.

Most veterinarians will give your dog a combination of two injections; the first one is a sedative, commonly propofol, which is what we use before we anesthetize animals before a routine procedure. This relaxes the muscles and slows down the heart rate and breathing.

Then they will give the euthanasia solution, an anesthetic drug. The vet will intentionally give too much of this drug so that your dog's brain forgets to tell the heart to beat and the lungs to breathe, and then he will quietly pass. This is why we call it "putting an animal to sleep," because essentially, that is what we are doing.

The veterinarian will listen to see if there is any heart activity, and they will let you know that your dog has passed. You can spend as much time with your dog after, and usually, you can leave when you are ready. If you need more time, take it; we know that you will probably never feel truly ready to say goodbye and want to give you all the time you need.

Sometimes the dog will need to get more of the injection; that is okay. It doesn't mean anything is wrong. Sometimes a limb or muscle will twitch; that is okay. It just means the pent-up energy in the muscles is leaving the body. Sometimes the dog will let out a sound or a big sigh; that is okay. It means the muscles of the chest and lungs are relaxing for the last time. Your

Photo Courtesy of Julie Russon

dog may urinate or defecate. That is okay; it's just the muscles of the lower abdomen relaxing. It is going to be devastating losing your best friend. It is the hardest part about owning a dog, and that is okay because you love him, and he loved you, and that is all that matters.

Burial and cremation

After your dog is euthanized, you have options about what you would like to be done with the body. Some people like to take their dogs home and bury them on their property. Buring your dog on your property is only permissible if it is allowed in your neighborhood and is legal at the city, county, and state level. There are some rules that require the pet to be buried a specific distance from a water source, a dwelling, or buried at a certain depth. Look into your local rules and regulations if you feel like this is your desired option. Others would rather have the veterinary staff take care of the body. There are two options that they can provide for you, a common cremation and a private cremation.

A common cremation is where you will not get your dog's ashes back. Instead, the crematorium will cremate your dog's body with other common cremations, and they will usually take the ashes and spread them somewhere locally. Many crematoriums have a memorial garden where they will do this. This is the cheapest cremation option.

A private cremation is where your dog will be cremated separately, the ashes collected, and then returned to you in a small container. This process usually takes a bit longer, but you will usually get your dog's ashes returned to the veterinary clinic within a week. The veterinary staff will call you when the ashes have returned, and you will be able to come by and pick them up whenever you are ready.

There is also the option to get a clay paw, which is an imprint of your dog's paw as a memento. These are great for shadow boxes or to stand up next to your dog's photo. Some people even use them as Christmas ornaments.

In addition to these services, you can choose a specific urn you would like your dog's ashes to be returned in for an additional cost, and there are also some companies that will make jewelry or art with the ashes of your dog in order to memorialize him.

These choices are very personal. I personally have had my pets individually cremated with the ashes returned to me, and I have created shadow boxes for my dogs with some of their favorite things, including their collars, toys, clay paw, and a framed portrait.

After the loss of your pet

Losing one's pet is never easy, and it can be harder for some than others. There are resources out there that can help specifically with the loss of a pet. Your veterinarian may already have some of those resources available to you. It is not crazy to feel very emotional over the loss of a pet. Some people have referred to their pets as their children, and their loss can be similar to losing a child. When I interviewed at a Specialty hospital in Colorado, they asked during my interview how people feel about their pets, I of course, said like their children. The interviewer said, sometimes, but a lot of people see their pets as an extension of themselves. Losing a pet can feel like losing a part of yourself. Your routine changes, the house feels different, a clash of changes all occur at once. It is okay not to do well during this time.

Look in your area for pet loss support groups. Many humane societies have these as part of their programming if you prefer in person. The Tufts University Cumming School of Veterinary Medicine has a Pet Loss Support Hotline that is available 6-9pm EST Monday through Friday, but also has 24hr voicemail. That phone number is: (508) 839-7966.

There are also internet-based support groups that can help you with pet loss and bereavement. These websites have everything from virtual condolence cards to Pet Loss Candle ceremonies and counselors. Some of these resources can be found at the following websites:

- **Association for Pet Loss and Bereavement - (aplb.org)**
- **Pet loss Grief Support - (petloss.com)**
- **Rainbows Bridge Grief Support Center - (rainbowsbridge.com)**

Oftentimes, friends or family members will ask if you are going to get another dog, and that is a question you don't have to answer right away. Everyone is different, and some people take a long time before they are ready for another dog, especially after having such an amazing, lively, infuriatingly brilliant dog like a Jack Russell Terrier. Some people go out and get a new dog within the next week after losing their pet. To each their own. However, when you are ready to start looking for a new dog, there are some things to remember.

- Make sure you have adequately grieved your lost pet. This will allow you to look forward to your new pet instead of constantly back at the one you just lost.
- Don't make a quick decision when considering a new pet. People may try to pressure you into a new pet, but only get one when you are ready.

- Make sure everyone in your family is ready and involved in the decision. Children may take longer to recover from the loss of a pet.

- Remember your next pet is not a replacement for the one you lost. You can never replace that relationship, no matter how similar they look or act.

- Consider your new pet as a fresh start or a new beginning. Learn from the mistakes you made last time, appreciate all you learned, and change any regrets into beautiful memories. A new pet is a new opportunity, and opening your heart to love again is one of the strongest and most beneficial ways we can grow.

I have lost a handful of dogs in my long history of being a dog owner, and the loss of each one has been vastly different. My grieving process was unique to each dog, and my readiness for a new dog was always variable. Luckily when I had my last dog die, I had Marty McFly to fall back on. It was a rough transition for both of us at first, but our bond has grown even stronger as we have both grieved together. It took me a year or two to realize I would be ready to add another dog to our home, but I have decided at this point, given Marty McFly's age and his chronic conditions, I am going to wait until he passes to make that addition. Instead, I am going to give him all my love and time I can and make these last years his best years.